ON THE TRAIL OF COFFIN MAN

Researching 19th Century Gravestone Carvers of Central New York State

Mary L. Dexter

ISBN 978-0-578-66350-0

Published by
Mary L. Dexter
Cortland, NY 13045

2nd Printing 2022

Front Cover: Center Cemetery, Cabot, Washington County, Vermont - Burial site for Jonas Stuart Sr. and his son James G. Stewart. Photo - Tina Utter; Inset: Texas Valley Cemetery, Cortland County, New York. Photo - Mary Dexter.

Back Cover: Top photo – Texas Valley Cemetery, Cortland County, New York; Left Bottom photo – Open Urn, Laceyville, PA; Tympanums: Angel - Eclectic Man, Heart - JW Stewart, Sun Rays - Sunburst Man. All photos – Mary Dexter.

About the Author: Top photo – Tina Utter. Other photos - Mary Dexter.

Table of Contents

DEDICATION

To the Memory Of
Shirley G. Heppell
1924 – 2005

It is with deep appreciation and fond remembrance that I dedicate this body of work to Shirley G. Heppell, librarian, historian, teacher, mentor and dear friend. Her encouragement and continuing support of a Bicentennial project (1975-1976) involving the Cortland County cemetery survey, resulted in uncovering a previously unknown gravestone carving family. Their eighteenth and nineteenth century, art in stones, was rendered and placed in central New York, Pennsylvania, Vermont, and New Hampshire. A perfect example of the way a valuable project can unearth previously unknown treasures.

ACKNOWLEDGEMENTS

Dale and Tina Utter to whom I am profoundly grateful for their being the champions of this book and carrying it to the finish line.

David Moyer for digitizing my original thesis. Randi Kepecs and Kathleen O'Connell who scrutinized multiple drafts of this book and whose advice, support and technical assistance improved the pages.

Members of the New York State Archaeological Association – Central New York State Cemetery Network for their inputs and encouragement.

I would also like to recognize the following friends and associates who contributed to this project in so many varied ways through their cemetery visitations, attendance at presentations, comments, questions and suggestions: Brenda Curtis, Rebecca Davison, Ann Dexter, Randy Frazier, Laurel K. Gabel, Marianne Greenfield, Kathy Greenia, Rose Halko, Linda Herrick, Peggy Jenks, Beth Kell, Terry Kerwin, Laurie Lindgren, Mary Lou McGuire, Kathleen O'Connell, Kurt Riegel, Dale and Tina Utter, Anita Wright.

Colin Sanborn and staff at the Fiske Library, Claremont, N. H.

Dale Storms and staff at Chenango County Historical Society, Norwich, N. Y.

University of North Carolina at Chapel Hill, Professors Joy S. Kasson, Daniel W. Patterson and Charles G. Zug, III. All three touched the original Honor's Thesis in memorable and special ways and I am truly honored to have studied with them.

FOREWORD

For some, the death's head and winged faces of the New England States were the pinnacles of early gravestone carving. The urn and willow iconography that followed was insignificant in comparison. Mary Dexter's thesis, which is Part One of this book, differs from that opinion and commences to dispel that myth.

Her studies of gravestones started with a simple Cortland County, New York cemetery survey in 1975 and blossomed into a passion for the early gravestone carvers of central New York. Part One of her book establishes the early history of Cortland County and the conditions that would allow these early carvers to flourish. She selects five local carvers for the focus of her research and then does an in-depth study on each of them. Mary uncovers a skill, creativity, diversity and originality within these carvers that clearly demonstrates they have earned their place in gravestone iconography and without a doubt should be appreciated in their own right as a valuable part of the history of gravestone art.

This passion and research which culminated in Mary's Honor's Thesis was completed in 1987 and is just as relevant now as when it was initially written. In addition, it lays the foundation for her expertise in this field and makes her the premier authority on the early carvers of central New York. But her work was not complete with this thesis. She continued on with her research and discoveries.

Part Two focuses on one of the five carvers that she depicted in her thesis she discovered during her 1975 survey. Her inquisitiveness propelled her into countless cemeteries looking at hundreds of gravestones and conducting research into probate records, historical societies, newspapers, and census reports. All of this to uncover the name of a carver she nicknamed Coffin Man. After twenty-three years her steadfast efforts were rewarded by not only discovering his name but that he came from a family of carvers from New Hampshire and Vermont. This knowledge only led to more questions and study.

Part Three tells of her efforts for the next fourteen years and portrays the rest of the story of this gifted gravestone carving family. During her travels she uncovered two carvers that left many unanswered questions. Slowly she unraveled the mystery and discovered that one appears to have been an apprentice to Coffin Man and is explained in Part Four. Another carver that is closely associated with Coffin Man we learn more about in Part Five. Through Mary's writings you will come to know the complexities of identifying one carver's work over another. The only way to know and truly distinguish a carver is by studying their unique lettering and designs.

This book is a culmination of 45 years of work and is the most comprehensive, if not the only recording, of some of the early carvers found in central New York. But Mary's work is still not complete. Each answered question generates more unknowns and pushes her to continue with her quest seeking even more knowledge on the gravestone carvers she has come to know so intimately.

It has been a privilege and an honor to assist Mary in putting together her life's work and making it available to the public so they too can benefit from her years of investigation. It is hoped this book will spur further interest and research into this obscure field of our early history.

Dale F. Utter
Editor

PART ONE

REMEMBER ME, AS YOU PASS BY:

The Early Gravestone Carvers of
Cortland County, New York

REMEMBER ME, AS YOU PASS BY:

The Early Gravestone Carvers of Cortland County, New York

by
Mary Louise Dexter

Honors Thesis
Interdisciplinary Studies Curriculum
University of North Carolina

1987

Revised October 2020

Approved by:
Charles G. Zug III
Advisor

CONTENTS

☞ **REMEMBER ME, AS YOU PASS BY:**

The Early Gravestone Carvers Of
Cortland County, New York

Crisscrossing the rolling terrain of Cortland County, New York, passing over its heavily forested hills or meandering across the crop-checkered valleys, the observant traveler cannot overlook the cemeteries that dot the landscape. Some lie on the crest of hills; others rest in isolation among a copse of trees ringed by plowed fields. A few are encircled by stone walls, wrought iron fences or barbed wire, taciturn and seemingly inanimate. Simultaneously exhibiting a haunting yet morbid beauty, these gardens of the dead do possess an ability to speak. To some they suggest only an inescapable fate, but to others the inscribed monuments reacquaint us with our historical beginnings and earlier cultural values.

Keeney Settlement Cemetery

It was during the 1960s, while engaged in genealogical research for people interested in their Cortland County ancestors, that I discovered the many volumes of cemetery "readings" on the shelves at the Cortland County Historical Society. The binders contain typed pages listing the name of the deceased, date of death and age, or any part of that information which could be abstracted from a tombstone. The records were produced by society members during the 1930s and 1940s and provide a valuable, condensed source of otherwise non-existent vital statistics.[1]

Occasionally I went to the sites to photograph particular gravestones of interest for a client. However, I found that some cemeteries no longer existed and that quite a few gravestones were now missing or were victims of vandalism. Still others were literally "flaking" or "melting" away.

Responding to a disturbing sense of impending loss, coupled with a desire to work on a fitting Bicentennial project during 1975, I initiated a re-inventory of all of the burial sites within my native county. Armed with information provided by the Historical Society records, I set out to pay a personal visit to each site and make a record of what I observed. Using a current map of the county, I carefully charted each location where gravestones were found or records confirmed that a burial had occurred. When located, I noted the general physical condition of the site as well as the earliest and most recent burial dates, took photographs, and when possible, determined the property owner or agency responsible for care and maintenance. Examples of exceptional iconography, types of markers, and curious inscriptions, epitaphs or other oddities that seemed significant were also chronicled. Nearly one hundred-fifty burial sites were identified, visited and inventoried over a two-year period.[2] (Appendix A)

For the next several years I spoke to a wide variety of organizations about various aspects of the county's cemeteries and worked to raise local consciousness concerning the urgent need to improve the physical condition of many of the sites. I sought out opportunities to locate those responsible for their maintenance, upkeep and protection. But as I worked and continually revisited cemeteries, many questions arose. I came to wonder how closely and in what ways the sites and the individual tombstones reflected and paralleled the county's changing social, economic, religious, and artistic culture.

The identity of the carvers tantalized me. What kind of artisan chiseled these monuments? Was he a local craftsman or traveling man? Was it his vocation or only an avocation?

I also puzzled over the types of stones used, a grey-brown rock that looked quite like the outcroppings seen throughout Cortland County and a soft, white marble whose surfaces today are distorted, discolored and nearly illegible. Was the former "slate?" And why were the marbles that often reflect later dates so worn away? If the earlier stones were more durable it seemed strange that they were replaced by the apparently inferior marble.

The iconography on the stones proved even more intriguing. On the earlier stones the symbols and images are far more individualistic, seemingly crude and non-uniform in execution. Nevertheless, they appear creatively expressive compared to motifs on later grave markers that offer less imaginative, repetitious designs. I wondered who chose the stone's motif, the family or the stonecutter? Did the symbols that complement the inscription tell us something about the deceased, the family, the community, or the stonecutter himself? What influences contributed to the design variations that the carvers used?

Attempting to answer these questions, I initiated a second survey of Cortland County's cemeteries in 1985. During another two-year period ninety-four sites were revisited within the county (Appendices B and C) as well as forty more locations in adjacent counties. (Appendix E) At each local cemetery I recorded pre-1855 grave markers noting the type of stone, name of the deceased, and the "name" or a "pseudonym" of the engraver if one could be determined.[3] In addition, I individually catalogued more than 500 significant sample stones, each was measured, sketched or photographed. (Appendix F) Some were rubbed to produce high-contrast reproductions for detailed study of the inscriptive and iconographic styles and techniques.

The earliest date within this survey was determined while visiting the Atwater Cemetery in the Town of Homer. A large, dark-brown, moss covered slab stands firm, solidly in the grasp of roots of an aged hemlock. It commemorates the 1795 death of a pioneer, white settler Keziah Alvord, and seems to be the county's earliest extant date recorded in stone.[4] During my earlier survey I had observed two carvers' names "A. Joiner" and "P. P. Moore." A subsequent check of federal and state census records revealed that these two craftsmen left the county between 1850 and 1855.

Initially I was naive enough to think that these two carvers had engraved the bulk of the dark stone monuments prior to 1855 and that the balance were probably the singular works of amateurs who produced a stone or two for members of their own family or neighbors. As my search began to locate the work of Joiner and Moore, I quickly became aware that there were many other craftsmen involved, each producing a body of work that reflected distinctive, identifiable styles and patterns. As I walked the cemetery rows from side to side and from front to rear, passing before these provocative, yet disarmingly mute stones, it became impossible to view their surfaces as casually as I had apparently done so often before. They now had so much more to tell me, so many questions raised and needing answers. But first I needed to learn their language in order to interpret their individual and collective messages.

Between the turn of the century and 1855 several thousand grave markers were set in Cortland County, these consisted predominantly of a variety of dark stone and white marble. My study concerns the former exclusively. This material was used for the earliest grave markers, most of which continue to display crisp, clear engraved imagery. In contrast, the marbles exhibit serious granular disintegration; therefore, they are only quantitative figures in the study. The only exceptions are noted in the list of stone carvers (Appendix G) where I have included all craftsmen whose names are still legible on marble gravestones dated 1855 or prior.

South central New York State is part of the Appalachian Plateau geomorphic province. Erosion of the ancient Acadian Highlands deposited clays, muds, silts, and sands westward so that in recent times, geologically speaking, sandstones comprise about twenty percent of the sedimentary rock volume (Heaslip 22). This sandstone ranges in texture from conglomeritic to exceedingly fine-grained with a very even finish. The slightly angular sand grains are tightly bonded by an indurated matrix of materials that produces relatively hard rock in a wide variety of colors ranging from brown and red to grey and blue. These desirable qualities of the native bedrock produced a local source of tombstone material.

The major drawback, then as now, is the layered nature of sandstone; shaping the top and cutting into the stone's surface exposes multiple layers. All exposed layered surfaces are sensitive to physical weathering. Rain and frost penetrate the layers and are frozen. Their expansion eventually causes splitting or "sheeting" along bedding planes. Exfoliation has been the primary contributor to the loss of the county's earliest gravestone art, but this process has been intensified over the years by human neglect, carelessness and misappropriation.

In seeking background material to complement my survey findings, I discovered that most existing studies focused primarily on New England gravestones (Benes, Forbes, Ludwig, Tashjian). The message they convey, with regard to the gravestones that stand in my locale, is that these monuments are of little interest artistically, culturally, or historically, since they fall chronologically "beyond the pale" of significant gravestone iconography and craftsmanship.

For example, the much-respected Connecticut gravestone authority Dr. Ernest Caulfield remarked, "We...found why [certain old graveyards] were deserted; they usually contained nothing but urn and-willow designs, the most uninteresting gravestones ever carved" (Caulfield 41). Art historian Allen Ludwig sees "New England stone carving [as] American art in quiet isolation" adding that "nothing of the older [stone carving] tradition remained after 1815 but silence of a forgotten epoch in our visual history" (Ludwig 428). Finally, Richard Welch views the urn and willow motif "as a step backward in gravestone art" that generally "lacks the visual interest and impact of the traditionally engraved stones" (Welch 68).

Significant iconography and superior craftsmanship are touted as the exclusive domain of New England artisans. It is authoritatively implied that "the art form" developed and flourished during the seventeenth and eighteenth centuries under the Yankee mantle and then died, quite suddenly, at the turn of the nineteenth century within New England's metes and bounds.

My Cortland County gravestone survey does not agree with this exclusionary theory. I daily viewed sculptured monuments that displayed creative, graphic interpretations of mortality and resurrection, themes certainly reminiscent of those viewed in the photographs, rubbings and illustrations of New England gravestones: winged soul effigies, wide-eyed faces, coffins, and imaginative variations of the willow tree, and Grecian urn motifs. Flowers, vines, and intricate geometric embellishments showed no lack of inventive originality. On the contrary, I found a multiplicity and diversity of personal styles that strongly imply that Cortland County's earliest stonecutters did not immediately succumb to the expediency of the times; their imagery and native vision continued to be inspired and highly individual at least until 1830.

After this date a more mechanized form of carving dominates. Thinly inscribed decoration, perhaps accomplished with stencil patterns, leads to more uniform design and precise measurements. The inscriptions become more deeply incised and suggest that the local carver's effort to distinguish himself was now restricted to inscriptive flourishes and layout. Finally, as mid-century approached, marble began to dominate; sandstone grave markers no longer found a place in Cortland County graveyards, and the craftsmen who designed, engraved, and created them took a step back into the footnotes of history.

This in-depth look at the work of Cortland County's earliest gravestone cutters is in response not only to my own initial curiosity about who carved the earliest grave markers, but also to a strong desire to refute the implication that there was no significant American folk art produced in the form of gravestones anywhere but within the hallowed halls of old New England. Cortland County's cemeteries can be counted among the growing body of regional exceptions to that supposition (Combs, Stokes, Trask, Welch).

In the ensuing essay I will discuss the county's formation and some of the social, cultural, economic, religious, and technical influences present in upstate central New York State during the first half of the nineteenth century that might help to explain the existence of this interesting body of early American folk art. I will then identify the gravestone carvers individually by delineating their design and stylistic variations.

The styles and motifs demonstrate an interconnectedness between local stone carvers and certain New England traditions. However, I hope to establish that there is ample evidence within Cortland County's burial sites to show that originality and creativity in American gravestone sculpture did indeed exist outside New England in the nineteenth century.

Tympanum - The top part of the stone above the finials or shoulders.

Iconography - In our area the iconography usually consists of an urn and/or willow.

Finials - These can be found on the top of both sides of the stone and are also called shoulders.

Inscription - This area contains the name, death and birth dates.

Epitaph - Often a bible verse, cause of death or other comments about the deceased.

Border - This is the design or detail work on the sides of the stone.

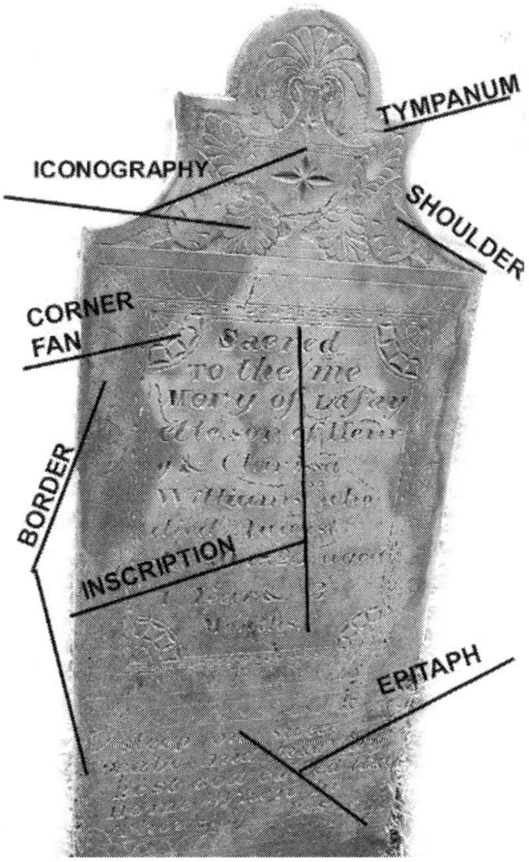

Endnotes

[1] The State of New York did not officially require vital records to be maintained by municipalities and towns until the 1880s, even then the response was erratic.

[2] I continued to use the number pattern established by the original Cortland County Historical Society cemetery reading project. Each site within each town was assigned a number starting at one. I have added a double-letter prefix to identify the particular town:

CN - Cincinnatus	HO - Homer	SO - Solon
CT – Cortlandville	LA – Lapeer	TA - Taylor
CU - Cuyler	MA - Marathon	TX - Truxton
FR - Freetown	PR - Preble	VL – Virgil
HA - Harford	SC - Scott	WL - Willet

The sites which lay in the Villages of Homer, and Marathon were numbered as if in those respective towns (which is physically the case.) The three sites in the Village of McGraw were assigned Town of Cortlandville numbers. The four early sites that lay in what is now the City of Cortland were not numbered since theoretically all remains and markers were removed to either the Cortland Rural Cemetery (CT-01) or St. Mary's Cemetery (CT-02). Remains and grave markers continue to surface from time to time. When referring to these former sites, I identify them by name. (See Appendix C for Town/Site locations.)

[3] In the largest cemeteries the pre-1855 marble stones were not counted due to the large area to be covered, the high number of stones and my time restrictions. Some sites also contain marble markers so badly disintegrated and weathered a date could not be determined.

[4] A notation in the Town of Truxton readings at the Cortland County Historical Society indicates that the date "1791" may have been on a stone at the burial site called "Pelham Cemetery" (TX-06). That marker cannot be found and little else remains at the site today except for a curious circular ground depression whose archeological significance has not been determined.

I. CORTLAND COUNTY

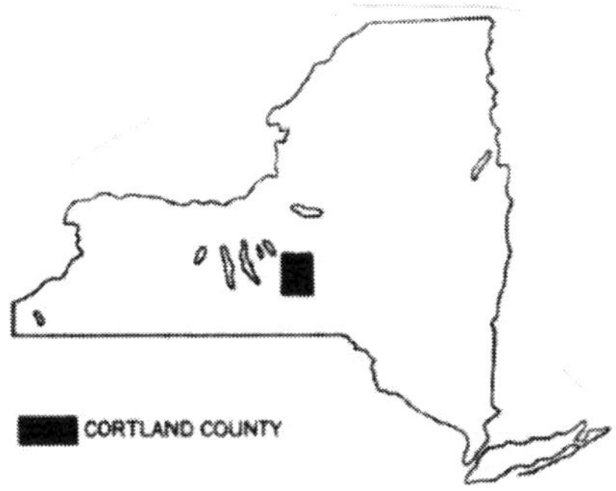

Situated in the heart of New York State, Cortland County lay in the wake of the New England migratory flood that surged westward at the close of the eighteenth century. It anchored the southeast corner of a nearly two-million acre "Military Tract," which the state opened for settlement following the Revolutionary War (Ellis 152-3).

The first permanent white settlers arrived in late 1791. During the three decades that followed, the state's population quadrupled, and the five hundred square mile area that is Cortland County increased to over 16,000 inhabitants. The migration was so dominated by New Englanders that Yale President Timothy Dwight commented that by 1820 the state was becoming "a colony from New England" (Ellis 189). He estimated that as many as two-thirds of the inhabitants had relocated from the northeastern states. Early county histories strongly suggest that the Cortland percentage ran higher, since foreign immigration was numerically insignificant before mid-century. Many with Yankee roots spent a generation or so temporarily settled in the New York counties adjacent to the Hudson River, anticipating the availability of abundant, cheap, fertile land previously held by the Iroquois Confederacy west of the Fort Stanwix Line (Ellis 152).

For example, farmer, merchant, and stonecutter David H. Manrose arrived about 1805 from Washington County, New York and eventually settled at Freetown Corners. During the pioneer decade; however, most settlers arrived from Massachusetts, Connecticut, and Vermont. The county's most prolific stonecutter, Vermont native Asa Joiner, migrated with his parents to the Virgil area when he was a young boy.

Although positioned at the leading edge of the rapidly expanding frontier, Cortland County rested between the major westward routes to the north and south. Its relative isolation from the main paths of travel and influence, and a perception that farmland was less fertile than the more distant valley of the Genesee, tended to retard settlement and development for a decade or so compared to surrounding areas. However, by 1808 a more rapidly growing population and a corresponding increase in local industry and agriculture was sufficient to encourage the Legislature to set off the southern half of Onondaga County as a separate entity. The newly formed county took the name of the state's first Lieutenant Governor, Pierre Van Cortlandt (French 250).

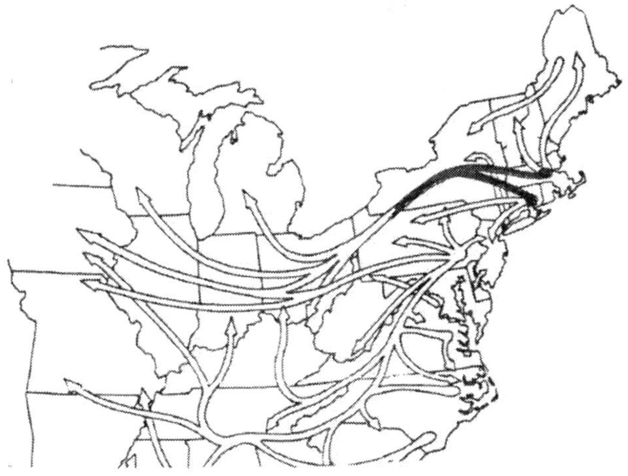

Routes/Patterns of Cultural Diffusion and Migration
(Glassie 1968, 38)

Timothy Dwight circumvented Cortland during his 1803 and 1815 "new frontier" travels, although he passed through adjacent counties with identical population bases. It delighted him to find that central New York wilderness towns had reproduced the church, the school and "the sprightliness, thrift and beauty of New England" (Dwight 25). Though sparse in numbers, the isolated but literate Yankees lost no time in setting up common schools, a few before 1800. The initial transplanting of Congregationalism in 1801 eventually gave way to predominantly Baptist, Presbyterian, and Methodist congregations (Ellis 196-8). By 1825 evangelical Protestantism dominated the culture.

The frontier population brought with them only the barest of necessities and experienced a decade of isolation and extreme self-sufficiency. The post-Revolutionary War period was one of high inflation and unstable currency. Hard cash was at a premium. Lacking ready money, the settler turned to barter with neighbors, payment-in-kind to craftspeople, or long-term credit to land agents or storekeepers.

For more than one hundred years agriculture formed the county's economic base. After the initial decade of survival and eventual attainment of a level of self-sufficiency, farmers sought to do better than simply break-even by marketing limited surpluses. Highways, crude in nature and limited in scope, served as the main arteries of transportation, but distances to external markets and high costs resulted in a minimum return for their efforts. With the flow of products in both directions stifled, waterways were touted as a viable alternative.

Near the tiny community of Cortland, on the Tioughnioga River, entrepreneur Elkanah Watson laid out a model port, and the high spring water carried marketable products southward from "Port Watson." However, the eventual key to agricultural prosperity in the region proved to be the construction of the Erie Canal which opened in 1825. Less than forty miles from most of Cortland's population, "Clinton's Ditch" markedly altered and improved the social and economic conditions.

In the New England tradition, town governments were organized very soon after the first plots were cleared. Local representatives appeared shortly in the Legislature and at the Constitutional Convention in 1821. By the 1830s the political domination of the state government by the landed aristocracy came to an end.

The predominantly Yankee population replicated their way of life and left an indelible imprint on the character and institutions of Cortland County. Just as they brought new life, they were also accompanied by death. It was not unusual for these earliest settlers to have to pick a burial site before choosing the school or church location. The cemetery served as one of the overlapping institutions which continued to reflect the strong New England cultural influence. However, there were important variations and modifications produced by the new, less confining environment.

For a century and a half New England settlement patterns dictated that the graveyard be located on, or adjacent to, the Town Commons. Land was scarce and prompted communities to remain close-knit for mutual protection and security. With westward expansion in the late eighteenth century, abundant land resulted in decentralization of the population and produced an alternative pattern. The result in Cortland County is a proliferation of family burial plots that dot the landscape, making up about 90 of the county's 150 sites. Only Homer and Cortland Villages were initially laid out in the traditional pattern with churches and public buildings bordering a "commons." In the mid-nineteenth century, the remains from both of these early village burying grounds were removed to new "rural" cemetery sites. All other "community" burial sites are found in the general vicinity of the original settlement but not central to it.

Fig. 1

Lacking a source of quarried stone or the funds to import it, an early choice for grave markers was either wood, which had limited durability, or local fieldstones. Most of the latter that remain in place are small and without notation of any kind, possibly due to a lack of tools or the skill to use them. An undisturbed cluster of these stones can be found in the Burlingame Cemetery in Willet (WT-02). A few fieldstones are crudely inscribed with initials or a date but otherwise lack decoration. An exception is the broken Jonathan Prince Potter fieldstone marker (1814) found along Lapp Road in the Town of Solon (SO-05). At the base break, there appears about half an inverted triangle with a partial interior design. The stone's base has not been found so that the puzzle can be completed (Fig. 1). The carver of the stone is unknown, but he does not appear to have been an amateur due to the controlled lettering and the decorative design choice.

Only two gravestones display a pre-1800 death date, and both were most probably backdated.[1] In fact, there seem to be relatively few completely inscribed stone grave markers prior to 1810 even though nearly 9,000 persons were residing in the county at that time.[2] My survey includes 101 burial sites and within that group are all of the earliest extant locations. I found only 14 gravestones with death dates prior to 1810 and speculate that this disproportionately low number may be due to the combination of wooden marker disintegration, fieldstone misappropriation, and accidental destruction or deliberate relocation of stones from sites no longer recognized or respected as burial places.

Still, there are adequate quantities of intact, legible gravestones remaining to provide ample opportunity to assess the work of some of the professional stone carvers who produced early gravestones for Cortland County's dead. By comparing their work with that of New England contemporaries I hope to learn more about the diffusion of styles, the innovative use of imagery, and the cultural changes which occurred in Cortland County.

Much has been written about the gravestones of New England and the men who cut them (Buckeye). There are endless arguments concerning nearly all aspects of that collection of early American sculpture, but there is general agreement on the three major iconographic phases.

The first focuses on the death's head imagery, skulls of both realistic and stylized natures (Fig. 2). Often leering from the tympanum through a double row of prominent teeth, this macabre image is sometimes accompanied by wings, crossbones, or a variety of secondary motifs such

Fig. 2

as the crown, hourglass, coffin, pick, shovel, and flowers. Initially appearing in coastal New England graveyards during the 1670s and 1680s, some scholars suggest that the icon was reflective of, or was a reaction to, orthodox Puritanism that dominated the culture. Espousing the doctrine of predestination, people looked upon death as a fearsome prospect; thus, the gravestone imagery focused on mortality.

Fig. 3

Replacing the death's head popularity by the mid-eighteenth century was the cherub, or soul effigy; a fleshed out, more angelic, softer-featured face, usually with wings (Fig. 3). During the preceding decades an intense religious revival movement occurred. The message of the "Great Awakening" was the gospel of salvation and new hope for redemption, individuals were believed to have more control over the possibility of their afterlife. The spirit/soul imagery now presented more human faces, and the designs more strongly expressed the hope of resurrection and salvation.

Fig. 4

During the 1770s and 1780s a third style appeared. Within a short span of years, the urn and willow dominated the sculptured designs decorating New England gravestones (Fig. 4). Further softening of religious attitudes coupled with a strong Continental influence based on the classical models of Imperial Rome and Olympic Greece swept across the "new republic." With an emphasis on nature and sentimentality, the neo-classical influence was reflected also in architecture, furniture, music, and art.

This sequential pattern of gravestone motifs is repeated in Cortland County, though my survey revealed no example of the death's head icon. The settlement of the county coincided with the waning period of the winged-cherub style when the New England cemeteries were displaying examples of the urn and willow imagery.

Fig 5.

There is a group of gravestones, found almost exclusively in the Town of Cuyler, particularly in the Keeney Settlement Cemetery, which displays large, stylized, linear, wide-eyed faces on the tympanum (Fig. 5). A few display a benign expression while the definite upturned mouth of others leaves no doubt the human-featured face is smiling. Although lacking wings, these figures are characteristic of the second phase of gravestone imagery. The carver's consistent use of the tripartite tympanum with a three-quarter circle lunette, as well as his alternate motif design of a geometric sunburst influenced my choice of "Sunburst Man" as a pseudonym. He produced what appears to be one of the earliest, fully engraved tombstones in Cortland County.

Fig. 6

Another body of work found in the county's southeastern towns repeatedly employs the stylized, empty coffin. This carver, pseudonymed "Coffin Man," uses this motif in combination with a simple linear willow. The box, nearly always standing on end, is generally centered at the base of the stone below the inscription, suggesting its purpose may have been both as a decoration and the artist's signature (Fig. 6). This carver is a contemporary of Sunburst Man. Their work however appears at opposite ends of the county. A third carver, labeled "Eclectic Man," whose work appears as late as 1828 also uses the simple, linear coffin in conjunction with a willow form. The coffin was a secondary icon used most often as a mortality emblem during the first style period.

The winged effigy, so popular in New England, makes a solitary appearance in Cortland County. Side by side in the Virgil Rural Cemetery (VL-01) stand a pair of reddish-brown sandstone monuments each displaying unique features within the county. One stone contains only a minimum of linear border decoration and a large, centered, numerical inscription "1824." The lunette of the companion stone exhibits double, winged figures. The pair of soul-effigies stares out at the viewer, wide-eyed and individually expressive, although neither could be said to be frowning or smiling (Fig. 7). The tiny wings protrude from the ear position and their interior design appears scaly rather than feathery. Beneath finely carved linear arches are two willow forms bending gracefully inward toward a centered geometric design, possibly a funerary urn. A double row of brick work completes the tympanum and appears again in multiple rows at the stone's base. The inscription is the detailed and lengthy commemoration of two sons of Ira and Sarah Woods. Both children died in 1823; therefore, the "1824" inscription might well be the year the anonymous carver completed the sculpture. Since the stone is unique, it may not have been produced locally.

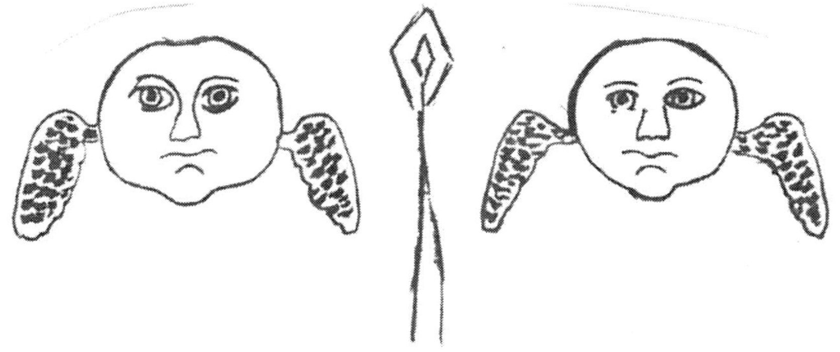

Fig. 7

There is a second, badly damaged stone by this same carver memorializing Philip Hopkins located a few miles away in a Virgil pasture. Close inspection of the remaining pieces does not reveal any winged figures. Only a similar large date "1822," the year after Hopkins' death, fills the tympanum. Thus, the Woods gravestone represents the only example of a winged figure in the county. The work of this stonecutter, as well as that of Sunburst Man, Coffin Man and Eclectic Man, reflects the imagery of earlier stylistic periods. Only Sunburst Man completely avoided the third period imagery. The iconography employed by the others resulted from a synthesis of earlier motifs with those of the neoclassical period.

It is reported that the faces of the two earlier periods disappeared from New England graveyards by 1810.[3] This circumstance is paralleled in Cortland County within fifteen years. The urn and the willow, used separately and in tandem, dominate the sculpture designs etched upon the sandstone and marble gravestones in the county to 1855 and beyond.

The urn and willow style is grudgingly acknowledged by New England gravestone connoisseurs but seldom complimented. The design is consistently relegated to the bottom shelf, the last sentences of a final paragraph or chapter. Of the three design styles, it is generally classed as the poor relation, "apologetic…easy to overlook [and] unexceptional" (George 94). The result of such blanket judgments has been to deprecate, berate, and encourage negativism toward an entire segment of gravestone art.

A close look at Cortland County's pre-1830 stones reveals craftsmen who utilized the urn and willow motif to produce individually unique styles and a diversity of designs which reflect each carver's creative ability. After 1830 there is a marked change. The carvers concentrate their abilities on the inscription rather than the decorative aspects. Eventually their carving skill and creativity is reflected totally in the lettering in such a way that the inscription doubles as the decorative feature.

In her seminal work, Gravestones of Early New England, Harriette Forbes commented that "as we study the stones… they gradually arrange themselves into groups. Each style soon becomes like the handwriting of a friend" (Forbes 16). Cortland County's pre-1830 carvers display personal styles that are both creative and idiosyncratic, they appear to have been non-conformists attempting to sustain traditional craftsmanship. In the following chapters I will introduce you to five of my many new friends and share with you what Sunburst Man, Coffin Man, Comma Man, Furn Man and Eclectic Man have related to me through their etchings in stone, about themselves and about Cortland County's early decades. (Appendix H)

Endnotes

[1] The Keziah Alvord stone (1795) stands in the Atwater Cemetery (H0-04), Town of Homer. The style of cutting and other features suggest that carver was David H. Manrose, who did not appear to be producing gravestones before the mid or late 1820s. The Eunice Holley Stone (1799) was cut by Coffin Man who worked in Cortland County between 1811 and 1820.

[2] The Third United States Census-1810, lists the total inhabitants of Cortland County as 8,868. Only the totals are available. I have been informed that the original record containing the county's first complete list of Heads of Household has been lost or destroyed.

[3] "Winged skulls as late as 1803 in Boston Cape Cod area" (Benes 167); "folk spirit themes in Vermont and New Hampshire as late as 1804" (Benes 193).

II. SUNBURST MAN

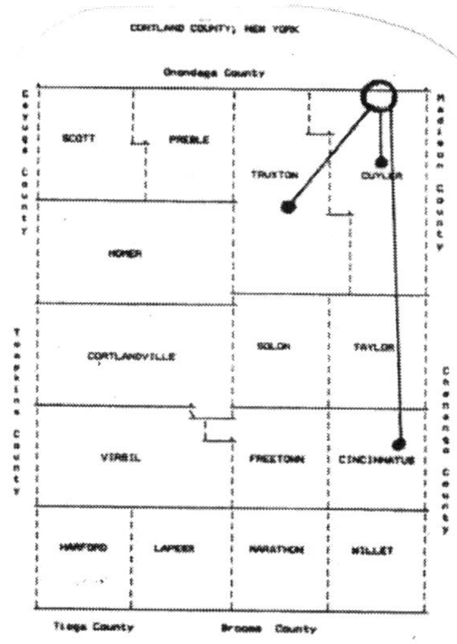

Thus far I have located only fifteen specimens of Sunburst Man's work. Their dates range from 1802 to 1823, and eleven (73%) are in the Keeney Settlement burying ground (CU-10), a relatively isolated site. None of these gravestones, nor any of the four others in three scattered sites further south in the county, is signed.[1]

Was this carver a resident of the town of Cuyler or Fabius or an itinerant?[2] Four of his stones exhibit some of the earliest dates appearing in the county. Can we consider him to be the first of the local gravestone craftsman? Where was he from and who or what influenced his iconography and the unusual lettering style? Close observation of his work will allow us to both speculate about answers to these questions and raise others, thereby building a foundation on which to launch a more in-depth future inquiry into his identity.

The physical composition of all fifteen gravestones is the same. Although similar in color to the bulk of sandstone markers in the county, the texture and construction of this carver's material is unlike the others. Only two demonstrate sheeting and both may have been broken as a result of a physical blow. All others show very little wear due to weathering and are currently resisting the tendency toward exfoliation. The stones are generally grey-brown in color with very uneven, undulating, pitted surfaces. The texture of the dressed face is smooth for the most part and seems to be considerably harder than other local sandstone. All of the specimens may have been quarried at a common site. Northern Cortland County embraces portions of the Tully Limestone Escarpment, and the stone adjacent to that geological phenomenon is different from the bedrock further south [3] (Heaslip 24). Locating the source of this unusual gravestone material could prove helpful.

Generally, Sunburst Man's gravestones as a group, are larger than the other pre-1830 carvers. When comparing the heights, I found that 71% of his gravestones stand over 37 inches out of the ground in contrast to an average 30% of the total stones of the other three carvers discussed. The tympanum shapes vary only slightly and this occurs at the shoulders (Fig. 8 a/b/c).

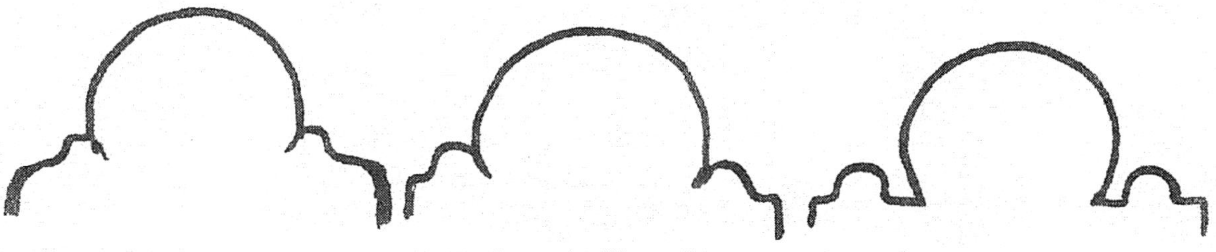

Fig. 8 a. b. c.

The incised designs and lettering are consistently thin-lined and shallow, quite possibly because of the hardness of the material and overall surface irregularities of the stone. However, in spite of the physical impediments, every aspect of the carvings manifests the superior qualities of a talented, skilled, meticulous and literate professional who took great pride in his craft.

A. Brown 1802

SFP Pettit 1812

Fig. 9 a. b.

Six of the extant thirteen images displayed within the tympanum crescent have almond-eyed faces; however, each is enclosed with a discriminating outline and head shape (Fig. 9 a/b). The variable mouth line ranges in expression from indifference to an unmistakable full smile. The tympanum border consists of either a convex scallop design or is left smooth occasionally inscribed with a thin line or two producing a subtle halo effect.

The balance of these grave markers displays variations on a geometric sunburst motif. Only one exhibits a 360° design, with twelve spokes emanating from a six-point rosette (Fig. 10). The others are half-suns, each with a different number of rays centered on a three-point geometric half-disc flanked by two smaller crescents.

Fig. 10

Both motifs are strong representations of the iconography of the second phase of New England gravestone imagery, although a search of available literature and image compilations has not revealed either of these particular designs as they are expressed in Cortland County. The spirit-image appearing on Achsah Brown's gravestone (1802) leaves no doubt about the ideogram's message, as the sharply upturned mouth infuses even the hollow eyes with an expression of joy and serenity (Fig. 9a). The epitaph complements the smiling icon with a religious message of comfort and resignation.

Twas from my god that I was sent
And to my parents I was lent
Unto my god I now return
Tender parents do not mourn.
(Achsah Brown Gravestone, 1802)

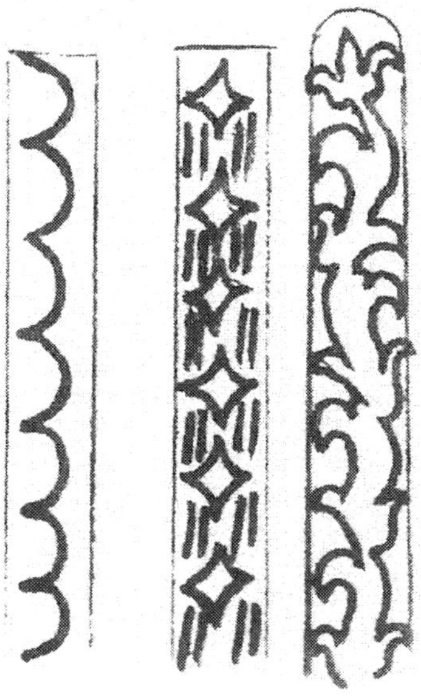

a. b. c.

Fig. 11

Sunburst Man's border designs vary in content. Many stones display a similar format whereby the side panels continue across the base enclosing both inscription and epitaph. When convex scallops are used to outline the tympanum then this pattern is continued down through the border panels. A leafy vine capped at the ends with a fleur-de-lis is another choice, but it is not extended upward into the tympanum like the scalloping (Fig. 11 a/b/c, 9 a/b).

Like the iconography, Sunburst Man's lettering is not like that of any other local carver, nor have I seen the style in New England commentaries. It is shallowly inscribed, oversize, and linear with Celtic flourishes at the extremities.

Capital letters, with a bar, display a point (e.g. A and H), the lower case "t" does not extend above half space and the old style "s" is used often. Individual letters, words and lines are precisely spaced, and often the carver adjusts the spacing so as to justify the inscription lines with the borders. Accurate spelling, correct grammar, and repeated use of contractions (electing an apostrophe in place of the vowel prior to a final consonant, e.g. Di'd, Expir'd) are all hallmarks of Sunburst Man's style. On one stone (SFP Pettit, 1812) the carver used the archaic forms "Aetat" to signify "age" and "SFP son to James."

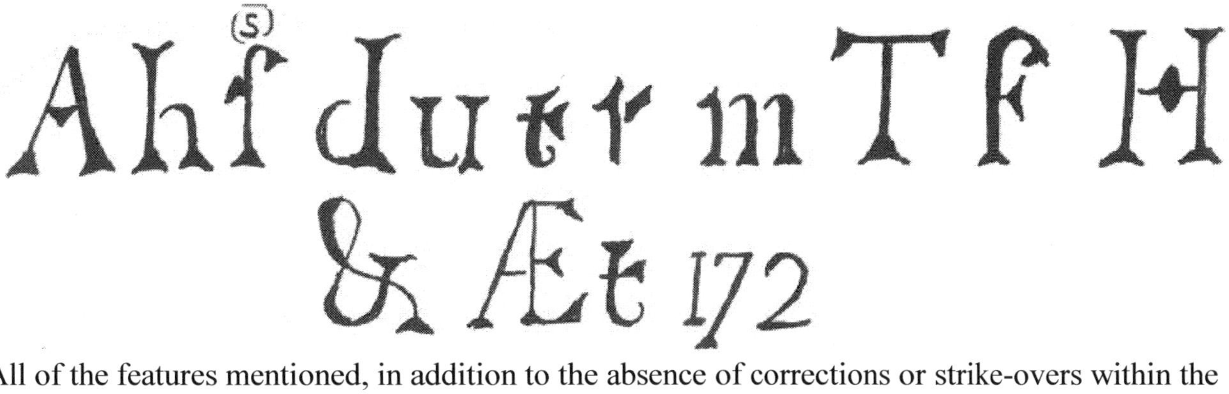

All of the features mentioned, in addition to the absence of corrections or strike-overs within the body of work, point not only to a meticulous craftsman but also to a very literate individual who excelled in subtle, creative variations of design.

The concentration of stones in the Keeney Settlement Cemetery and northeast Cortland County, and the lack of similar markers in adjacent counties, strongly suggest that Sunburst Man was a resident of the immediate area, most probably of the valley settlement itself. However, the continuing oral history traditions about the area do not produce even the slightest hint of a "stonecutter" among them. Perhaps he was a resident of the Onondaga County Town of Fabius, although to date, none of his work has been located further north.

The range of death dates connotes a twenty-year span of work, but a comparison of the dates with the iconography and consideration of adjunct inscription information on one particular stone provides some evidence to suggest that Sunburst Man probably arrived after 1810 and produced gravestones for only a little over ten years.

In 1812 two gravestones were needed by the Pettit family. The tympanum of each displays a face as does each marker needed in the succeeding years of 1813 (1), 1815 (1) and 1817 (2). The next year two grave markers display the half-sun motif. After a hiatus of four years, markers are again needed in 1822 (l) and 1823 (l) and sun-rays fill the crescent. It is evident that the face motif preceded the sunburst.

<u>INVENTORY</u>: (Site Key – see Appendix C)

Date	# Stones	Motif	Name	Adult/Child	Sex	Site
1802	1	Face	Brown	C	F	CU-10
1803	1	Sun	Risley	A	F	CU-10
1806	1	None	Bacon	A	F	CU-10
1809	1	?*	Whitmarsh	C	M	CU-09
1812	2	Face	Pettit	C	M	CU-10
		Face	Pettit	C	F	CU-10
1813	1	Face	Kingsley	C	F	CU-10
1815	1	Face	Benson	A	M	CN-01
1817	2	Face	Cadwell	C	F	CU-10
		Face	Beebe	C	F	CU-10
1818	2	Sun	Blanchard	A	M	CU-10
		Sun	Herrinton	C	F	TX-01
1822	1	Sun	Cadwell	A	F	CU-10
1823	1	Sun	Hoskins	A	F	CU-10
18 ?	1	?*	(possibly Keeler)	?	?	CU-09

*Damaged

Exhibiting a sunburst, the tombstone for Sally Risley bears the date 1803. Information about the Risley family is inscribed in lieu of a conventional epitaph. "A stillborn infant by her side" insinuates that the deceased died in childbirth. The reader then learns that her husband Waite remarried soon after to "Polly," by whom he had two sons who did not survive, "Noah di'd June 1806 [and] Wait di'd October 1811." The lengthy epigraphical addition is well executed, not crowded in, and appears to have been incorporated into the stone's original overall design. Considering the last date in the addendum, I feel reasonably certain that the Risley marker (1803) was backdated. The sunburst motif suggests that the carving more likely occurred sometime after 1817 when Sunburst Man's choice of iconography changed to that design.

What about the "1802" Brown grave marker manifesting the wonderful smiling face? The limited resources of the Brown family for several years after their arrival would strongly hint that they had little with which to compensate a professional gravestone cutter for providing a very large, handsome tombstone for their daughter until many years had passed. It would seem more likely that the Brown marker, like the Risley stone, was also backdated. Since a smiling icon fills the lunette of her gravestone the stonecutter probably carved it between 1811 and 1817 in his earlier "face" phase.

Sunburst Man closed out his stone carving career in Cortland County sometime after the spring of 1823 when Mehitable Hoskins died. Since there is no progression of design development or engraving quality, I assume that this stone carver arrived in the central New York area as a mature, skilled craftsman. His origins may lie in Connecticut. There is speculation that Sunburst Man's work resembles certain gravestones in Litchfield County, Connecticut associated with a craftsman referred to as "The Canaan Cutter."[4]

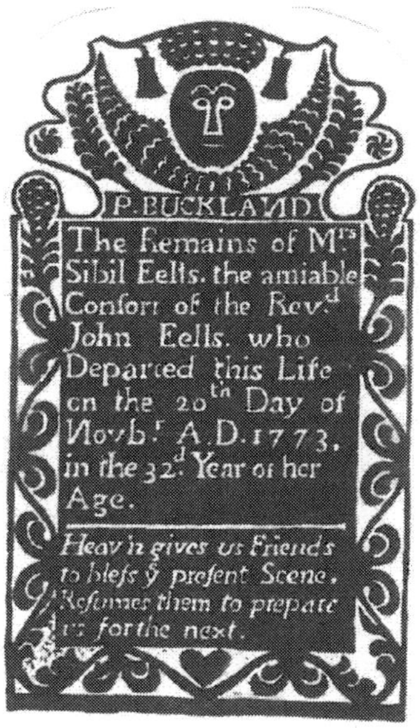

Fig. 12

Among the earliest settlers into the valley were five families from East Hartford, Connecticut. Arriving in 1795/6 they included Simon Keeney, Jr., his father, as well as Benjamin and Dorinda Brown whose only daughter Achsah's death in 1802 resulted in "the first grave in [the] cemetery" ("Meet…"7). In addition to the Browns, Sunburst Man's patrons also included the Cadwells, Bacons, and Risleys, all emigre families from the Connecticut Valley.

Was this stonecutter from central Connecticut? Do his abstract effigies, borders, lettering and occasional odd finial placement reflect an awareness of Hartford stone carver Peter Buckland and his Connecticut Valley disciples (Fig. 12)?[5]

At the top of the hill, in the back row of the Keeney Settlement Cemetery, stand a pair of Sunburst Man's monuments commemorating two of James and Lucy Pettit's children. Although epitaphs appear on many of his stones most are variations on commonly quoted verses with two exceptions—the Pettit stones. The words engraved are strikingly singular and constitute extremely personalized commentaries.

An infant son, "SFP," died in April of 1812, his very brief earthly sojourn is vividly recalled in stone (Fig. 13a). His six-year-old sister, Lucy, then died in August. Her unusual epitaph reads: (Fig. 13b)

Fig. 13a

She's gone! and to
My phrenzied mind
Rush'd wild impatience,
Doubt, distrust,
Religion whisper'd,
Be resign'd,
To take they idol
Hence, was just.

Fig. 13b

Why were these two grave markers chosen to exhibit such unusual atypical verse? The messages are emotionally charged and convey the impression of an intimate knowledge of the individuals involved. Who chose these words, the carver or the family? Might they have been one and the same?

James Pettit's origin is not known for certain; however, the 1790 Connecticut Federal Census lists only four families by that surname--all residing in Litchfield Township.[6] If the stones in the vicinity of Litchfield, Connecticut, do in fact look like Sunburst Man's work, then James Pettit may be the man to consider when continuing this search.

Endnotes

[1] Keeney Settlement Cemetery (CU-10), (11) stones; Cuyler Village Cemetery (CU-09), four miles south, (2) stones; Truxton Village Cemetery (TX-01), eight miles southeast, (l) stone; Cincinnatus Village Cemetery (CN-01), twenty miles south, (l) stone.

[2] Fabius, in Onondaga County, was one of the original "Military Tract" towns (ten miles square.) Its name, like other Tract names, including Virgil, Homer, Cincinnatus and Solon locally, reflect the late 18th century neoclassical fervor that took America by storm. At the time Cortland was set off from Onondaga County, the southern half of the Town of Fabius was renamed Truxton. In 1858 that town was again politically subdivided, the eastern half designated Cuyler. The Keeney Settlement Cemetery lies on the west side of the West Keeney Road. The east/west, county/town line intersects the graveyard and the Keeney Valley.

[3] For about one hundred miles across upper central New York State lies a band of very hard, medium-grained, neutral gray limestone sandwiched between beds of sedimentary, soft shales and sandstones. The Tully Escarpment winds across the northern towns of Cortland County and is a primary factor contributing to the topography of the area (Heaslip 24).

[4] Telephone conversation 3/11/87, Laurel Gabel, Association of Gravestone Studies, Research Coordinator.

[5] Peter Buckland (1743-1816), Hartford stonecutter, is said to have strongly influenced gravestone iconography in the Connecticut Valley. He is said to have developed the basic soul effigy design as a "common post-revolutionary style" that was used by other craftsmen in his area (Welch, 63).

[6] 1790 Federal Census for Litchfield Twp., Litchfield County, Connecticut, contains the names of four Pettit heads of household: Joel, John, Saml and Solomon. These families comprise all of the Pettits in that state. Several families are noted in Massachusetts, the name is very common in New York State. Genealogical work is called for, the carver seems to have a connection to James Pettit.

III. COFFIN MAN

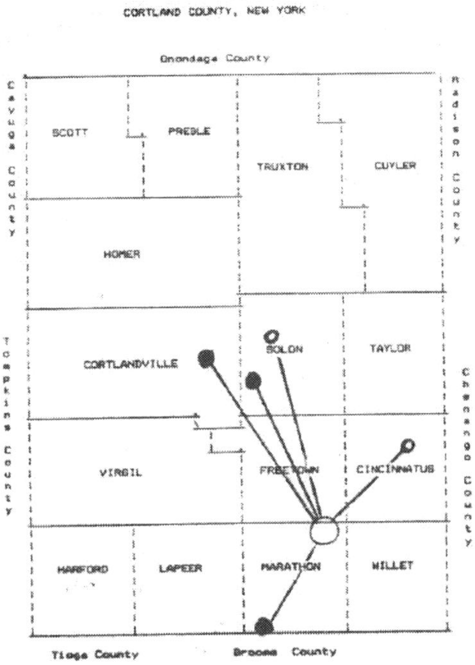

Lying predominantly in the eastern and southeastern towns of Cortland County are twenty-eight gravestones attributed to Coffin Man. More than half stand in the Texas Valley Cemetery (MA-02) and these fifteen constitute every pre-1820 marked burial at that location except one.[1] The balance of his work is scattered among five other county sites.[2] When the initial concentration of markers were noted in Texas Valley, I considered that the carver was a resident of that community, the distribution pattern within Cortland County favored that assumption. Further searching; however, revealed a wide distribution across three other New York counties to the south and east including Broome, Chenango and Delaware.

Coffin Man's actual date range in Cortland County runs from 1799 through 1820, but the concentration occurs during the century's second decade. The 1799 date appears on the marker carved for the first wife of Joseph Hawley.[3] "Eunice Holley" was buried in the Bingham family plot (SO-05).[4] Hawley, an early neighbor of Bingham's, eventually settled in the vicinity of Texas Valley where his second wife, Jedidah, died in 1816. Subsequently, he engaged Coffin Man to carve her gravestone (Fig. 15). During the years between the deaths of these two women, Hawley's economic circumstances presumably improved, and it seems probable that he also commissioned a stone for his first wife at the same time. The 1799 stone predates the balance of the carver's work by more than ten years and therefore is believed to be backdated (Fig. 14).

Fig. 14

Fig. 15

INVENTORY: (Site Key - see Appendix C)

Date	# Stones	Motif	# Base Coffins	Name	Adult/Child	Sex	Site
1799	1		1	Holley	A/A	F/F	SO-05
1811	2	Urn/W	2	French	A/C	F/M	MA-02
		Urn/W	?	Dwight	A	F	CN-01
1812	2	?	1	Barto	A	F	MA-02
		Urn/W	None	Rockwell	A	M	CN-01
1813	2	Urn	1	Johnson	A		MA-02
		?	1	Leach	A	F	MA-02
1814	2	Willow	2	Handerson	A/C	M/M	MA-02
		Urn/W	1	Bemis	A	M	MA-05
1815	1	Urn/W	2	Edwards	A/C	F/?	MA-02
1816	6	?	?	Lovell	C	F	MA-02
		Willow	1	Fish	A	F	CN-01
		Willow	1	Rankin	A	F	MA-02
		Urn/W	None	Whealock	A	F	CN-01
		Willow	1	Hawley	A	F	MA-02
*		Urn/W	2	Upham *	A	F/M	MA-02
1817	2	Urn/W	?	Wolsey	A	M	SO-01
		Urn/W ?	1	Smith	A	M	MA-02
1818	2	Urn/W	1	Hotchkiss	A	F	SO-05
		Urn/W	1	Robinson	A	M	CN-01
1819	7	Urn/W	?	Abbe	A	F	SO-05
		Urn/W	3	Tuttle	A/C/C	F/?	MA-05
		Heart/W	2	Barto	C	M/M	MA-02
		Urn/W	1	Leach	C	M	MA-02
		?	?	Lowe	C	M	MA-02
		None	?	Thompson	A/C	F/?	SO-05
		Urn/W	1	Kingman	A	M	CN-01
1820	1	Urn/W ?	?	Rice	A	F	CT-04

* Stone reads 1816: probate records confirm death 1817
? Information not available or cannot be determined
Urn/W = Urn/Willow

The carver's gravestone material is predominantly a gray-brown, medium-grained sandstone whose uniformity of color and texture suggests a single quarry site quite probably outside Cortland County.[5] There are also examples of the iron-oxide red tint sandstone among his work. The majority (74%) are medium-sized, standing 20 to 36 inches out of the ground, 57% are 1.5 inches or less thick. The quality of the sandstone and his beveling technique is such that remarkably very few of his markers exhibit any deterioration due to sheeting, except where subjected to careless maintenance or vandalism.

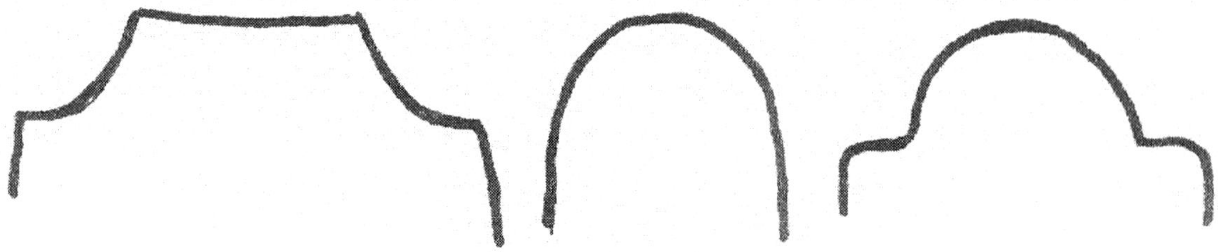

Fig. 16 a. b. c.

The carver did not utilize the tripartite configuration for his tops. There are no finials. In keeping with the overall design's simplicity, the tympanums range from flat to fully rounded; most are a combination of these forms, a half-round set between right-angled shoulders (Fig. 16 a/b/c).

Coffin Man's personal carving style can only be described as that of eloquent simplicity. He made full use of the neoclassical mainstays, the urn and willow, and his imaginative interpretations manifest a notable degree of creativity. The tympanum designs are not repeated within the county. Of the twenty gravestones displaying iconography, the majority (70%) are variations on the urn motif often in conjunction with a radically simplified willow (Fig. 17 a/b/c/d).

Fig. 17 a. b. c. d.

Three of the gravestones exhibit abstract variations on the willow motif (Fig. 18 a/b/c).

Fig. 18 a. b. c.

Rarely is there an opportunity to learn, with any degree of certainty, just how these early cutters personally interpreted the written word in stone. Since a three-branched "bush" image appears both in a tympanum and elsewhere on Coffin Man's local work (Fig. 18c), it was enlightening to have him “tell” me just what this symbol represented.[6] Among his repertoire, he viewed this graphic specifically as the "tree of life" and not simply as a leafy, decorative filler.

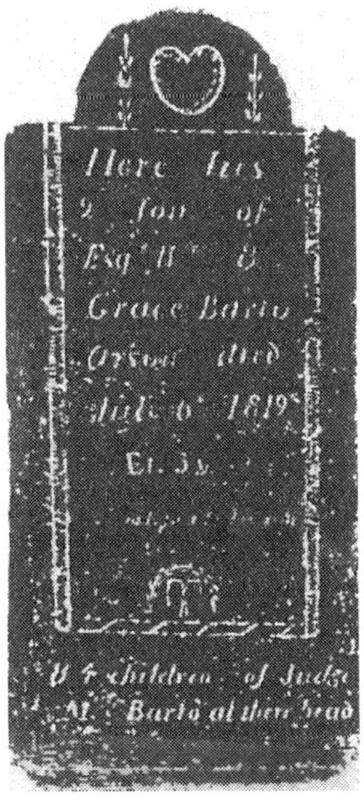

Fig. 19

Two markers present alternate themes. Three abstract six-point stars grace the Eunice Holley stone, and a large heart flanked by a pair of straight-line willows decorates the top of the gravestone erected to mark the resting place of six Barto children.[7] Although not proportionally oversized, the heart nonetheless dominates the stone visually (Fig. 19). Viewers are compelled to return their gaze to the figure at the top, this is true for most of this cutter's work. What is so captivating? What qualities create this attraction? The strangeness of some of the abstract urns possibly, but the heart holds the same compelling fascination. The carver very effectively used a minimum of incised lines to elicit a maximum surface effect. The overall designs are simple, open, uncluttered, and manifest a powerful balance and restraint.

There are no borders in the usual sense. He used a narrow band with an incised zig-zag pattern to outline the inscriptions. The design is alternated at times with a rope pattern.

The inscriptions are well executed in terms of spacing and uniformity of lettering. Like the iconography, there continues to be a simplicity within the inscription, both in the linear construction of each letter and the information provided. Nearly all inscriptions commence with the words “Here lies”, two begin “In Memory of” (Fig. 19a).

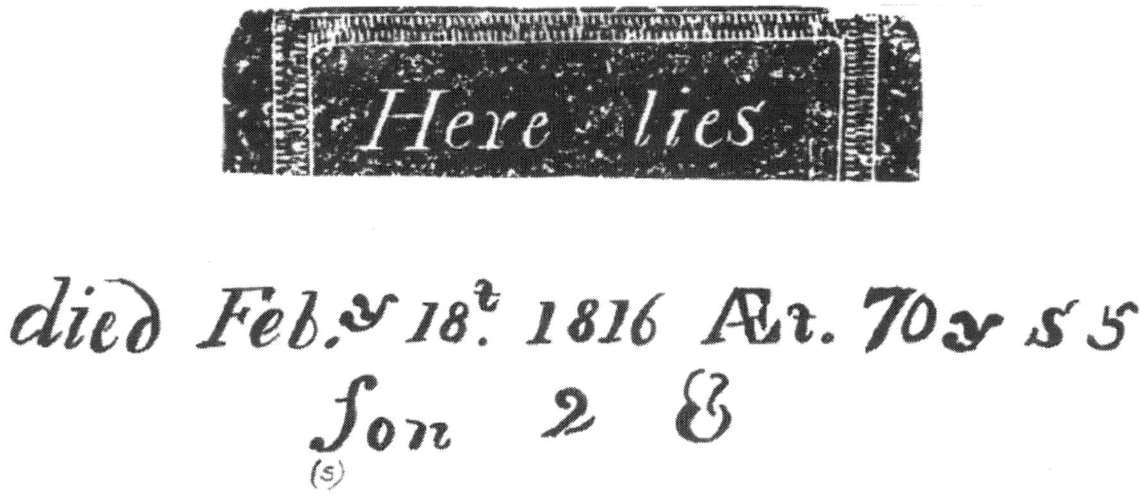

Fig. 19a

All the engraving is shallowly inscribed. The incised vertical lines of the letters evidence double width and an angled strike which produces subtle shadowing. The numbers are the same size as the capital letters. Short curved-line flourishes are found on many stones in order to fill and balance a line. 

There is seldom an epitaph. In Texas Valley only the Lydia French (1811) stone reveals any added sentiment and this is in the form of a biblical quote from Proverbs: "Who can find a virtuous woman, for her price is far above rubies." This grave also has a footstone, rarely found to survive among Coffin Man's work. The adjunct marker displays the notation "grandson at her feet" and a coffin beneath the deceased's large cursive capitalized initials. Only three footstones were found accompanying Coffin Man's headstones. An upright coffin at the base of a headstone is this carver's trademark, although its exact significance is uncertain. Of the twenty-eight markers surveyed, nineteen (68%) exhibit the upright coffin at the base, always sheltered by an arching, linear willow. Seven have multiple images indicative of more than one individual memorialized by the marker (Fig. 20).

Fig. 20

Fig. 21

The bases of five of the twenty-eight stones cannot be viewed due to natural barriers. Considering the high percent of fully exposed stones bearing coffins (83%) there is reason to believe that most of these five also display the emblem. One stone has no base imagery, another displays a horizontal linear willow and a third manifests a small urn with vaulting willow, an appropriate, compatible nineteenth century substitution for the coffin.

The number and size of the coffins coincide with the deceased being memorialized and thus physically represent the interred (fig. 20). In this way the symbol, particularly in conjunction with the "Here lies" salutation, expresses continuity with the mortality emblems and themes associated with the initial phase of New England gravestone art--the reality of physical death. The alternate introduction, "In Memory of" gained popularity during the second phase. A modified version, "To the Memory of" appeared with the neoclassical era, reflecting the sentimentality and restraint of the period. Coffin Man occasionally elected "In Memory of," never "To the Memory of." The archaic forms were preferred (Fig. 21).

It may not have been his deliberate intention to use the base coffin as his personal symbol; however, since he did not place his name or initials on any stones this device has become Coffin Man's graphic signature.

Why did this carver, in the early nineteenth century, feel such symbols were necessary beyond the words of the inscription? Although on one occasion he used an urn and willow as a digression from the coffin at the base of a marker, I am curious as to why he so faithfully persisted in using the coffin. He was obviously aware, as evidenced by the tympanum's urn and willow motifs he carved, that those were the preferred decorative themes. The old and the new are perceptively and skillfully interwoven. Coffin Man epitomizes the transitional stone carver.

Prior to 1820, it appears that the southeastern portion of Cortland County had access to only one gravestone cutter - Coffin Man. Why did the community of Texas Valley patronize him when the nearby settlements of Willet and Marathon did not? Was he close at hand or passing through on a regular basis? Were there relatives or former neighbors living in the area? His foray into the center of the county, two sites in the Town of Solon and in the Village of McGraw, may have been the result of a one-time visit late in the decade. The catalyst could have been Joseph Hawley's request for his first wife's gravestone after 1816. Coffin Man's three other stones at the Lapp Road site bear 1818 and 1819 dates. A single stone bearing the date 1817 lies in the nearby Greenman Cemetery (SO-01). Another is a short way down the road in McGraw Village (CT-04), where tree roots firmly anchor the Anna Rice (1820) marker. Might all six of these gravestones been carved at one time, in 1820? What is certain, is that the emergence of a new decade marked the end of Coffin Man's presence in Cortland County.

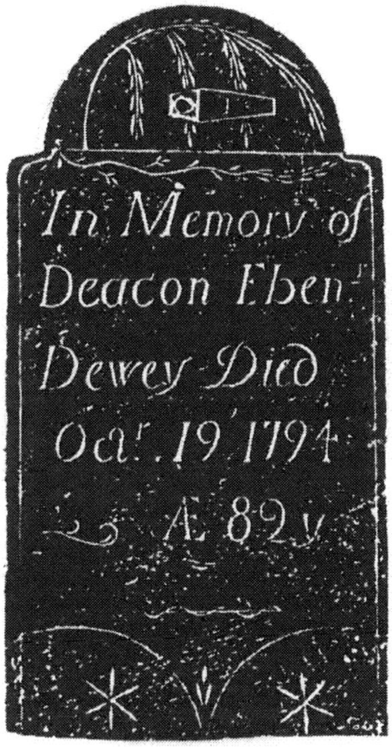

Fig. 22

Who was he? His exact identity eludes me but evidence currently leads me to believe that he came out of eastern central Vermont. A rubbing appearing in Edmund Gillon's collection reproduces a stone for "Ebenr Dewey", 1794 (Gillon, Plate 121). The volume failed to identify the location but called attention to the coffin, with face-inset, on the tympanum and the size of the stone. The shape and size of the marker, the coffin, placement of the willow branches behind the icon in addition to the distinctive lettering strongly suggested to me that the gravestone was cut by "Coffin Man" (Fig. 22). The location of the stone was not known then; however, the 1790 Vermont Federal Census lists two Ebenezer Deweys as Heads of Household in Royalton Township, Windsor County. The name does not appear in any other state for that year (Heads…1790). Until the Dewey stone and others like it are located this theory will remain speculative.

Thirty additional stones by Coffin Man have been located in the counties to the south and east of Cortland, and I am sure these areas hold more of this carver's work. The dates correspond generally to the same decade of his Cortland work. There is no sequential pattern relative to their locations; therefore, his residence remains a total mystery at this time. From the information available we can only conclude that he was an itinerant stone carver who worked in south-central New York State during the second decade of the nineteenth century as far west as eastern Cortland County.

Endnotes

[1] A marble marker dated 1816 for Dorathy Totman is presumed to be backdated work.
[2] Cincinnatus Village (CN-01), (6) stones; Tim Hill (MA-05), (1) stone; Lapp Road (SO-05), (4) stones; Greenman Cemetery (SO-01), (l) stone; McGraw Baptist Cemetery (CT-04), (l) stone.
[3] Hawley family information located in the "Hawley Genealogy File" at the Cortland County Historical Society, Cortland, New York.
[4] Johnson Bingham, a resident of Shaftsbury, Vermont and Anna Johnson, his wife, both natives of Connecticut, were the first settlers to arrive in what became the Town of Solon. The death of a daughter in 1798 established the first burial place in Solon at a "sacred spot on that old farm" according to information contained in the "Bingham Genealogy File" at the Cortland County Historical Society. For more than twenty years neighbors were buried in that plot on the Bingham family farm.
[5] The color of the stone is unusual for Cortland County. Since many of the carver's stones lie to the east that may also be the source area for this very light grey sandstone.
[6] In the Masonville Cemetery, Delaware County, N. Y., rests Joseph Bicknell, Esq. who died in 1817. His grave marker was cut by Coffin Man. The epitaph reads: "Blessed are they that do his Comdt that they may have right to the tree of life." Directly beneath these words is this illustration; a symbol that also appears on several other stones which he carved.

[7] The stone's inscriptions are for "Orson" and his brother, sons of William and Grace Barto. An addendum reads "4 children of Judge M Barto at their head" which connotes a common grave and leaves the rest to speculation. The two possibilities which come to mind include four infants, the result of a multiple birth or the remains of four children of varying ages, possibly killed in a fire.

IV. COMMA MAN

Fig. 23

While engaged in a study of the Little York community, I was mapping the grave positions and recording tombstone inscriptions in the small cemetery (HO-05). My probe struck a stone lying less than an inch below the surface. Its outline suggested a footstone so it was uncovered. I was in error. It was a small, dark grave marker exhibiting a large, eight-point, geometric rosette in relief that nearly filled the tympanum. Encased in each of the rounded shoulders was an incised spiral. Two thin-lined, minimal weeping willows were placed at the top and base. The semi-cursive lettered inscription appeared within a circle-in-relief, highlighted at the edge with incised dots which also accented the stone's borders and epitaph (Fig. 23). The letters were shallowly cut, and the epitaph was a classic example of phonic spelling:

"Soo faides/the Blooming/flower Cut down/& witherid in an/ower--"

When the stone was rubbed all the lettering became more legible. It was only then that I observed the multiple "commas." There are eight backward commas seemingly dispersed at random throughout the inscription which remembers "Olive A Grow," an infant daughter of Elisha and Lois Grow, who owned the property where they buried their child in 1827 (Fig. 24). It was in this setting that I was first introduced to Comma Man. Later, while doing fieldwork for this study, it became apparent that excessive punctuation appears on many of this stonecutter's gravestones.

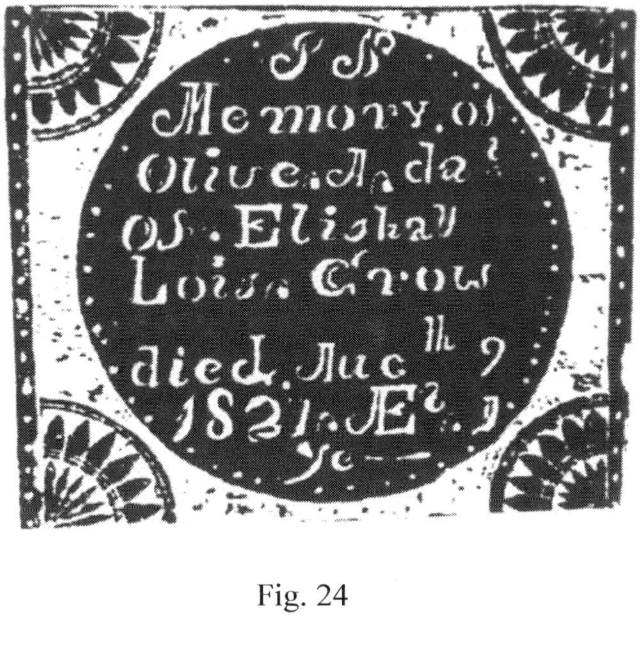

Fig. 24

Eighteen Comma Man tombstones have been located in Cortland County. These are widely scattered among the towns and do not demonstrate any strong patterns. There is a concentration of sorts found in the Town of Cuyler where eight gravestones are divided equally between two sites, Cuyler Village (CU 09) and Keeney Settlement (CU-10).[1] The date range for Comma Man's work starts in 1816 and runs through 1828.

INVENTORY: (Site Key – see Appendix C)

Date	# Stones	Motif	Name	Adult/Child	Sex	Site
1816	1	Willow	Allen	C	F	CU-09
1818	1	Urn	Hills	A	F	CU-10
1820	2	Urn	Jennings	A	M	MA-05
		?	Blancher	A	M	CN-01
1824	1	Willow	Allen	C	F	CU-09
1825	3	Urn	Hills	A	M	CU-10
		**	Fish	A	M	CN-01
		Willow	Young	C	F	PR-05
1826	4	U/W	Kingsbury	A	F	LA-08
		**	Keeler	C	F	CU-09
		U/W	Blanchard	C	F	CU-10
		U/W	Jennings	A	F	MA-05
1827	3	U/W	Risley	C	M	CU-10
		Geometric	Grow	C	F	HO-05
		Geometric	Beach	C/C	F/F	WL-02
1828	3	Urn	Allen	A	F	CU-09
		Willow	Crofoot	C	F	PR-05
		U/Vine	Morse	A	F	CU-09

** Inscribed by Comma Man but decorated by Furn Man

The three earliest dates appear on stones with surnames and familial connections on later monuments (Allen, 1816/28; Hills, 1818/25; Jennings, 1820/26). A fourth marker (Blancher, 1820) shares not only a somewhat isolated site with one other later dated stone (Fish, 1825), but the color and texture of the two pieces appears to be identical. Three to four years intervene (1820-1824) before the dates resume with consistency.

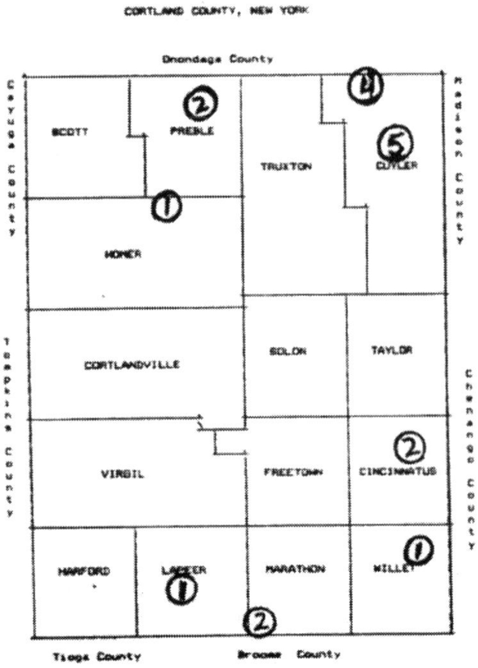

Considering these factors, I assume the earliest dates appear on backdated work, and the major production period commenced about 1824/25 and ran at least until 1829.[2] The tops of Comma Man's stones represent a variety of shapes; however, these might more appropriately be viewed as variations on a theme. The majority demonstrate the classic, tripartite "bed-board" style with a preference for finials so common among New England burial grounds. Sandstone does not lend itself to curved shapes due to its inherent layered structure which resists all but the tabular form. Comma Man's training and background must have been in an area where this technical accomplishment was mastered. Graceful curving independent finials were attempted with some visual success (Fig. 25a); however, most are now broken or remain in place only with braced support. As an alternative, several stones reveal a compromise created through the illusion of independent finials. He achieved this form by carving an inward spiral with graduating depth into the stone's partially rounded shoulders. The cut was not incised completely to the back (Fig. 25b). The effect is also attained when he inscribed spirals in the rounded shoulders (Fig. 25c).

Fig. 25 a. b. c.

Comma Man's iconography reflects an exciting, creative interpretation of the urn and willow motif, whether each component is used independently or in tandem. At times the willow appears as a bold hieroglyph, both incised and in relief (Fig. 26 a/b).

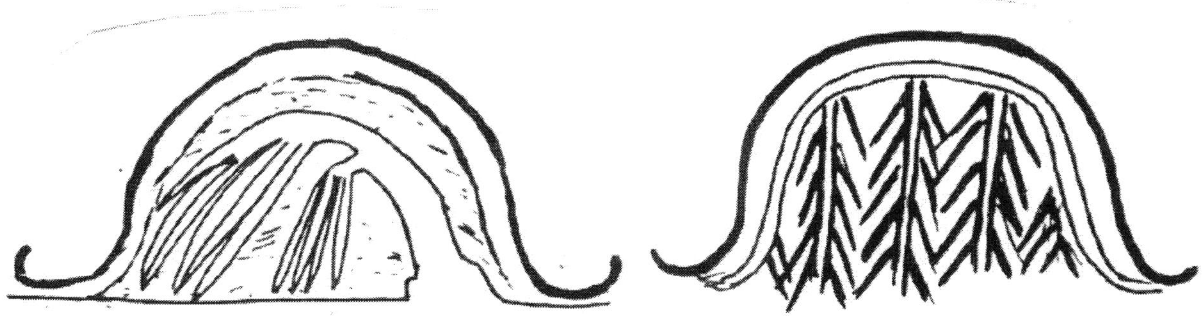

Fig. 26 a. b.

Alternately, it is executed in such a way that a herringbone drapery effect is the result. When combined with an urn, both these interpretations are featured again but always with creative modifications. The urns are usually elongated and quite unlike the classic Grecian receptacle (Fig. 27). Each exterior design is a unique geometric construct with minimal interior decoration, some stand in relief while others are delicately incised. Nearly all spew some form from the top opening: willows, a leafy vine, a spiral disc. A few of the urns appear in tandem with five or more small, plain balls connected to the receptacle's opening and to each other (Fig. 27c). Their significance eludes me. Are they flowers permanently at the grave?

Fig. 27 a. b. c.

The spiral disc occurs randomly among Comma Man’s grave markers, and he used it in a variety of ways. When appearing in pairs the spirals are engraved so as to “spin” in opposite directions. Another secondary form he employed repeatedly is what I have construed to be his “tree of life.” The shape is displayed most often in multiples, usually across the base of the monument, always bending as if in response to some undetected wind (Fig. 28).

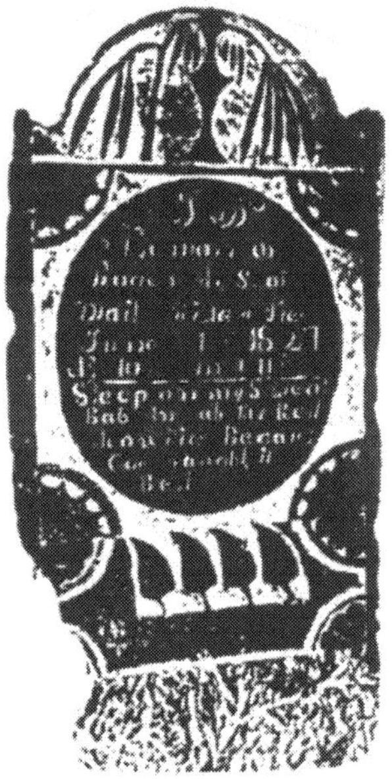

Fig. 28

There are no border panels per se. The Olive Grow marker has a series of dots, while some others manifest the herringbone willow or a double scallop. All are incised so lightly that they are often nearly undiscernible.

Fig. 29

The stone carver's inscriptions are distinctive for a number of reasons that make it difficult to confuse his work with anyone else's. Generally, the inscribing is very shallow and poorly spaced. Usually starting with “IN Memory of,” the predominant feature being the over-sized “IN”. The “I” bears resemblance to other cutters; however, in Cortland County the “N” belongs only to this carver (Fig. 29). Upper and lower-case letters are used although not always appropriately. He elects, without pattern, to choose letter style variations within an inscription and the size of his letters fluctuates within words throughout the production period.

There are some letters and numbers that are inscribed quite consistently and by dint of their unusual form, application, and repetition are helpful in identifying the carver's work.

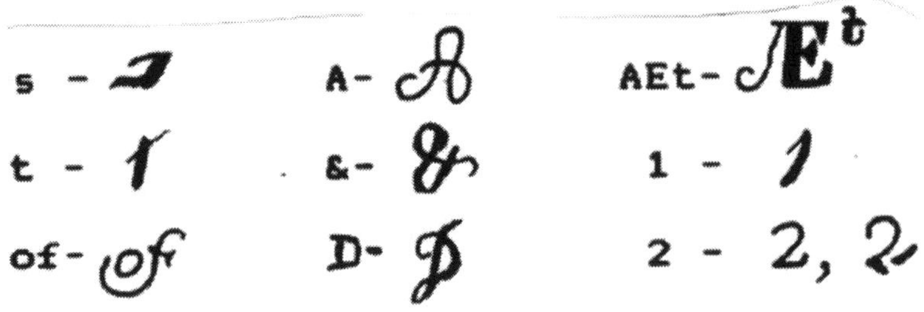

The excessive use of the comma on more than one third of his work (a colon is substituted on the Lorry Morse 1818 marker) does not connote ignorance of proper grammatical usage as I first thought. After studying each example, I determined that the comma is placed only between interior words and numbers, never at the beginning or end of a line. The carver selected punctuation forms to separate the words of the inscription. In one instance he placed the comma after nearly every word in the epitaph as well.

pra,cast,a,look,upon
this,tomb,a corpse,must
preach today by one,Sudin
blow,I,left,the,world,of
wo,to,tred,the,corts
above
(Job Blancher, 1820)

The irony here is that if one deletes the comma/colon, we find that Comma Man never used any punctuation whatsoever, not even the period. Ludwig comments that excessive punctuation and guidelines were used throughout early New England inscriptions but that colon separation went out of style around 1730. This "process of elision," in his opinion, was retained only by less-advanced, non-progressive carvers. He later qualifies this judgment by adding that "the need to punctuate was so great, however, that from time to time throughout the eighteenth century many rural stones... [broke] out in an epidemic of dots" (Ludwig 287).

Comma Man worked primarily with a dark grey, inferior sandstone. The dressed surface on which he engraved lengthy inscriptions and epitaphs is pitted and irregular, often with sizeable depressions. A few carvings appear on a lighter, finer grained sandstone; therefore, he may have acquired the stones from multiple sources and various means. One such instance makes this quite apparent. On two gravestones he cut the inscription but the iconography is the work of Furn Man. (See Inventory **) The color, texture, and overall design of the stone are consistent with that stone carver.

The relationship between these two craftsmen remains unknown. A comparison of their iconography and lettering reflect no similarities with the possible exception of a preference for finials. I will speculate that the families of the deceased may have had the decorated, uninscribed grave marker in their possession. When needed they were inscribed by Comma Man.

There is nothing within this carver's work that has offered a clue as to his residence or origin. His technical abilities are erratic and his literacy skills suggest only a basic education, but these qualities should not disqualify his work. His originality and inventiveness far outweigh any perceived mechanical or intellectual deficiencies.

Endnotes

[1] Cincinnatus Village (CN-01), (2) stones; Tim Hill Road (MA-05), (2) stones; Currie Road (PR-05), (2) stones; Highland Road (LA-08), (l) stone; Little York (HO-05), (l) stone; Burlingame Cemetery (WL-02), (l) stone.

[2] Comma Man's work appears outside Cortland County in DeRuyter, Madison County, four stones; Chenango County where three have been located; several in Upper Lisle in Broome County. One stone cut by Comma Man in the Upper Lisle Cemetery immediately south of the Cortland County line, is inscribed "1829," the latest date noted thus far for this carver in the area.

V. FURN MAN

The most prolific of Cortland's earliest stone carvers is a craftsman I have designated Furn Man. The pseudonym is a composite term to reflect the three primary motifs displayed, sometimes singly, more often in combination: the urn, fern and flower.

Within the county I have catalogued fifty-three grave markers located at twenty-one burial sites.[1] Like his contemporaries, Furn Man did not sign any of the work thus far discovered. All of the stones, with one exception, rest in burial sites throughout the county excluding the southwest towns.[2]

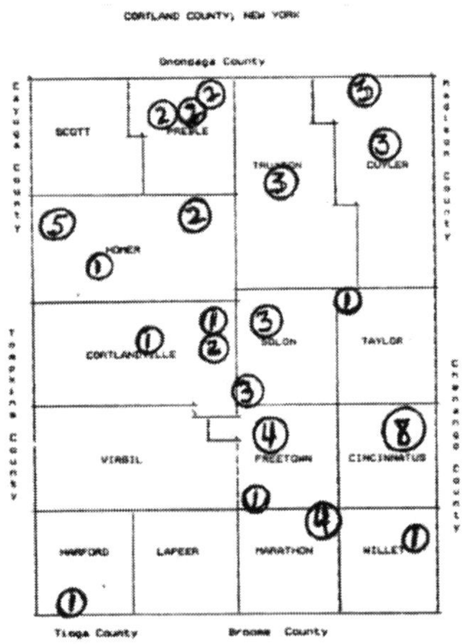

The actual date range begins with 1808 and ends abruptly with five monuments exhibiting death dates between March and late May 1828. Two of the earliest markers (Van Hosen, 1808 and Keeney, 1809) are companion works of later monuments for spouses, 1815 and 1817 respectively; therefore, the earlier stones are presumably backdated. Subsequent grave markers do not produce any obvious patterns to suggest an actual production period of less than 1810 through the spring of 1828. With few exceptions, the quantity of stones per year averages three, then in 1823 the number rises to seven. This peak is followed by a year in which not one grave marker by this cutter has been found.

Again, in 1826, when seemingly at his zenith in both quantity and quality of design, only one stone presents itself. This may have been a result of his absence either from the area or simply from the trade due to other commitments.

INVENTORY: (Site Key – see Appendix C)

Date	# Stones	Motif	Name	Adult/Child	Sex	Site
1808	2	?	Phelps	C	M	PR-03
		Urn/Willow	VanHoesen	A	F	PR-01
1809	1	U/W	Keeney	A	M	CU-10
1810	3	U/W	Alvord	C	M	HO-04
		U/W/Spiral	Alvord	A	M	HO-04
		U/W	Smith	A	F	HO-02
1812	1	Leaf/Vine	Alvord	A	M	HO-04
1813	5	Urns/Flwr	Davis	C/C	M/M	PR-05
		U/W	Harris	A	F	CU-10
		Urn	Smith	A	M	HO-02
		?	Walter	?	F	HO-04
		U/Flwrs	Walter	A	M	HO-04
1814	2	U/W	Keeler	A	F	CU-09
1814		Urn/Fern	Wartrous	C	F	FR-04
1815	3	U/Flwrs	Kinne	A	F	CT-07

		Urns/Vines	Keeler	C/C	F/F	CU-09
		Urn/Willow	VanHoesen	A	M	PR-01
1816	2	?	Smith	?	F	PR-03
		Flower	Sloan	A	F	TX-01
1817	2	U/W/Moon	Keeney	A	F	CU-10
		?	VanHoesen	3C	M/F/M	PR-05
1818	1	Willow	Burdick	A	F	HA-01
1820	3	Urn	Blanchard	A	F	CN-01
		U/W	Bush	C	F	TA-06
		U/Flowers	Keeler	A	F	CU-09
1821	2	Willow	Herrinton	A	F	TX-01
		U/Fern	Hull	A	F	FR-04
1822	4	Urn	Capron	C	M	SO-05
		U/Tendrils	Cowles	C	F	CT-03
		?	Dewey	A	F	HO-01
		?	Frink	A	M	CT-04
1823	7	?	Brush	A	F	TX-01
		U/Flower	Chappel	C	M	CN-01
		U/W	Dwight	C	M	CN-01
		?	Greenman	C	M	SO-01
		U/W	Greeman	C	F	SO-01
		Urns	Randall	C/C	F/M	SO-05
		U/W	Randall	C	F	SO-05
1825	4	Urn	Atwood	A	F	SO-01
		U/Fern	Lowe	A	M	MA-02
		U/Thistle	Conger	C	M	FR-04
		Ferns	Shepard	C	M	FR-04
1826	1	Urns/Flwr	Dwight	A	M	CN-01
1827	5	U/Flwr	Alvord	A	M	CN-01
		U/Frns/Sprls	Leach	A	M	MA-02
		Urn	Fish	A	F	CN-01
		Urn	Graves	C	F	CT-03
		Urn	Wheelock	A	F	CN-01
1828	5	U/Spirals	Jones	A	M	MA-02
		U/W	Rockwell	A	F	CN-01
		U/Flower	Curtis	A	M	FR-01
		U/Flower	Leach	A	M	MA-02
		U/W	Place	C	M	WL-02

? Motif undetermined due to damage

The sandstone material this stone carver used is fine-grained, presenting a very smooth surface on which he engraved his designs. The color is consistently light to medium grey with tonal variation of grey/green to grey/ochre. Sixty percent of the markers fall in the medium sized range (20-36 inches), but a third measure more than 37 inches above the ground.

Only one basic tympanum shape was used and only four stones present the single variation, that of pseudo-finials. A narrow, smooth border frames each marker, usually traversing the stone horizontally at the shoulders to divide the tympanum and inscription (Fig. 30a/b).

Fig. 30 a. b.

The classical urn dominates the iconography. Always resting on a pedestal of different shapes and heights, the motif is centered under the lunette's semicircular crown and usually decorated with one or two stars within the bowl and neck. At times a horizontal decorative band crosses the bowl. Sprouting from most urns are willows, ferns, single or double flames, leafy vines or an assortment of flowers (Fig. 31). Any of these motifs may also be found flanking the vessel.

Fig. 31

The willow accompanies the urn. Its broad trunk rises on the left side and arches into the crown where individual branches full of leaves cascade behind and to the right of the receptacle (Fig. 32). The natural looking tree and foliage contrast starkly with the abstract linear interpretations of the other early carvers. I did not find a willow as an independent motif.

Midway through his production period a variant type of foliage appears--a long, narrow, leafy fern, at times either pointed or rounded at the extremity. Lightly inscribed dots and lines provide interior definition. In general, Furn Man was not disposed to leave spaces unoccupied. The fern itself is presented as the central motif on the Shepard (1825) marker (FR-04) (Fig. 33). In the same cemetery the Polly Wartrous tombstone displays the entire inscription within a large urn cut in relief, the tympanum filled with fern fronds.

Fig. 32

Fig. 33

Fig. 34

The pedestal also serves as a casement for an hour-glass, a symbol seen most during the first phase of New England imagery. Geometric side fans and brickwork at the base complete the gravestone design (Fig. 34).

A variety of flowers appears in Furn Man's work, each blossom seems unique. In the Truxton Cemetery (TX-01) the central motif on the Delia Sloan grave marker is a single bloom encircled by a small-leafed vine (Fig. 35/36). Philodendron-shaped leaves complement the central motifs, fill the base of some stones or appear as borders to the stone or to the inscription.

Fig. 35

Fig. 36

No particular border designs predominate when space was allowed for such decoration. A variety of repeating, geometric, linear patterns is common. Occasionally a simple rope design serves as both the stone's border and the outline of the inscription.

Furn Man's inscriptions consistently begin with "In Memory of" and are incised to a medium depth producing well-defined letters and numbers. Both upper and lower-case letters are used, capitals appearing somewhat randomly. Punctuation is sparse and usually limited to the period at the end of the inscription and epitaph. The words are cut to fill a given line; thus, it is not unusual that the deceased's name and/or the date are split, falling on different lines. In most instances, the first word "In" is cut larger than any of those that follow and the "I" is always larger than the "n." On some gravestones, "In Memory" appears in a curved, banner-like orientation, at times arching over a sunburst design.

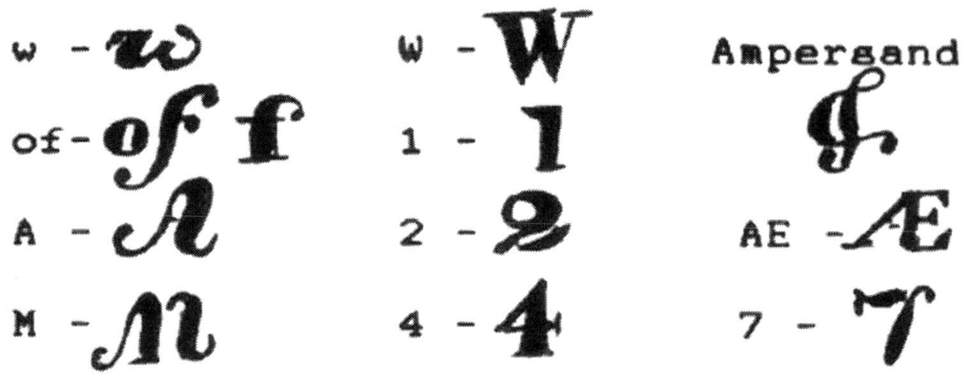

Many of the tombstones carry standard verses. A few are personalized to reflect the name of the deceased or the circumstance surrounding the death.

Only four footstones have been located, all small and with a rounded top. They contain the deceased's initials and are without decoration except for the Albert E. Shepard 1825 marker. His initials are contained within the yang/yin symbol (Fig. 37).

Fig. 37

Quite a few of Furn Man's stones are damaged, several are broken in half or at the base. Others display a totally or partially fractured tympanum. Whether caused by vandalism or careless maintenance, the predominant contributing factor is the thinness of the stone itself. More than 70% were found to be 1½ inches or less thick. The innate structure of the sandstone is also promoting irreversible damage. The particular grade of stone that Furn Man chose was not only fine grained but exhibits multiple narrow layers as well. Incising the face of the stones with his extremely ornate designs and electing to shape the tops in the manner he did commonly exposes the multiple layers to the elements. Moisture and precipitation, followed by freezing and thawing, work to separate the layers, causing the faces to sheet off. Furn Man's largest stone, that of Captain Alexander Leach (1827) (MA-02), stands today in imminent danger. The first layer containing all of the engraved design has separated completely from the ground to the shoulders. That portion literally hangs free, secured only at the top. Its precarious situation and fragile condition make the possibility of producing a rubbing a high-risk proposition. Between visits in 1985 and 1986 I discovered that the lower right portion has broken away. The rest cannot be far behind.

There are certain characteristics that suggest this body of work may have been produced by more than one cutter. The inscription lettering varies slightly, although there are some stones that reflect all the variations. There seems to be a technical proficiency in the decorative engraving that does not continue through into the inscription or epitaph. The carver's work falls into two distinct sequential groups, the earlier stones in the northern towns and the later dated grave markers in the southern towns of the county. The design differences are subtle and, like the lettering, there are some markers with combination motifs. If this is not the work of one carver with a broad repertoire within the urn and willow theme, then the two or three men who crafted these monuments certainly seem to have been associated in some way, possibly in a common workshop. Comma Man did inscribe at least two gravestones which Furn Man decorated; however, their styles are quite distinctive.[3] Only when every one of the stones is photographed in detail, under proper lighting conditions, will it be possible to differentiate among the stones with any degree of certainty. My records are not that complete at this time.

Fig. 39

Fig. 40

Fig. 41

Overall, Furn Man's work is ornate and the technical skills displayed by this engraver of stone are exceptional. The symmetrical imagery and vertical geometric border panels suggest stenciling; however, close examination of the engraving reveals definite size variations. No two monuments are exactly alike, and although there are a few geometric corner or side fans that appear regularly, the overall designs reflect creative arrangements and a multiplicity of formats. There is a fluidity and gracefulness coupled with balance that cause these monuments to catch and hold one's attention. As evidenced by his gravestones, he was a skilled, well trained, professional stone carver (Fig. 39).

Edmund Gillon's book of New England gravestone rubbings include the William Abbot grave marker (Plate 124) whose iconography and lettering bear a striking resemblance to Furn Man's work, particularly the Sabrina Randall gravestone (1825) in the Lapp Road Cemetery (SO-05) (Fig. 40 & 41). The author does not provide a location for the Abbott marker; however, I presume it lies somewhere in New England. It appears that Furn Man is another migrating Yankee craftsman and the relationship between the carver of the Abbott stone and Furn Man is worth investigating.

Endnotes

[1] Between one and four stones in each of these sites - Town of Cortlandville: Conable Cemetery (CT-07), McGraw Rural Cemetery (CT-03), Old Baptist Site (McGraw) (CT-04); Town of Cuyler: Cuyler Village Cemetery (CU-09), Keeney Settlement Cemetery (CU-10); Town of Freetown: Galatia Cemetery (FR 01), Freetown Corners Cemetery (FR-04); Town of Harford: Harford Cemetery (HA-01); Town of Homer: Glenwood Cemetery (HO-01), East Homer Cemetery (HO-02), Atwater Cemetery (HO-04); Town of Marathon: Texas Valley Cemetery (MA-02); Town of Preble: Elmwood Cemetery (PR-01), Town Garage Site (PR-03), Currie Road Site (PR-05); Town of Solon: Greenman Cemetery (SO-01), Lapp Road Cemetery (SO-05); Town of Taylor: Gay Family Cemetery, (TA-06); Town of Truxton: Truxton Rural Cemetery (TX-01); Town of Willet: Burlingame Cemetery (WL-02).
The Cincinnatus Village Cemetery (CN-01) contains seven stones assigned to Furn Man.

[2] The Lorry Burdick gravestone stands in the Harford Cemetery (HA-01) in southwest Cortland County.

[3] Two stones decorated by Furn Man, inscribed by Comma Man:

Allen Fish	1825	Urn/W (CN-01)
Rachel Keeler	1826	Urn/W (CU-09)

VI. ECLECTIC MAN

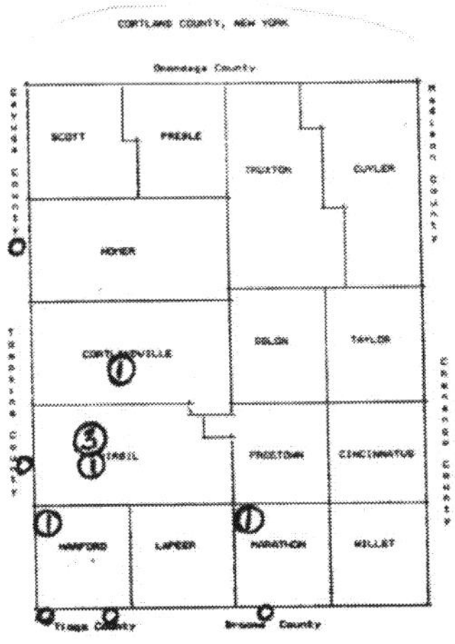

To date, only seven examples of Eclectic Man's work have been found in Cortland County, and two are fragments. The tombstones are located primarily in the southwest portion of the county, four at the Virgil Village sites and one each in very isolated family plots in the Towns of Harford and Marathon.[1] The most recently discovered example was unearthed in a residential area of the City of Cortland, and I believe it once stood in the original Cortland Village Burying Ground, now a city park adjacent to the courthouse.[2]

Eclectic Man's range of dates fall between 1808 and 1826 although there is evidence to suggest that the two earliest stones may not have been produced until about 1823.[3]

INVENTORY: (Site Key – see Appendix C)

Date	# Stones	Motif	Name	Adult/Child	Sex	Site
1808	1	Urn	Luce	A	M	VL-02
1813	1	Urn/Willow	Roe	A	M	VL-02
1816	1	*	Crary	A	F	CT-x
1821	1	Steeple/Willow	Ball	A	M	VL-01
1823	1	Steeple/Disc	Terry	A	M	MA-06
1824	1	Urn/Willow	Carson	A	F	VL-02
1826	1	Urn/*	Norwood	A	M	HA-03

* Tympanum broken off and not found

The sandstone is of varying quality and texture, the color being predominantly reddish brown which suggests relatively local sources. There is no consistency in size, which ranges from one only 27 inches out of the ground and 1 inch thick to a 48-inch stone some 2 ½ inches thick. The shape of the markers is basically the half round lunette centered between right-angled shoulders, although in keeping with his style, there are variations (Fig. 42 a/b).

Fig. 42 a. b.

In addition to the urn willow and coffin, a wide variety of images can be found within the very small range of this carver's work. His designs include: foliated forms, steeples, a bird, a ship and a trumpeting angel. There is a degree of asymmetry within the stones which gives the impression that Eclectic Man literally “created” his gravestones as he carved.

Fig. 43

The central figure on four of the markers is a stylized urn. The bowl is decorated with swag lines, leafy scrolling, and simple linear flourishes. The long neck, scored with diagonal hatching, is narrow and finger-like with the tip curving slightly to the left. The base of the pedestal graduates into an arch, then the lines fall vertically to form a frame to enclose the inscription. The iconography and the inscription are enhanced by narrow zig-zag patterns producing an unusual visual effect. The background color tones are deepened, so that the urn, arch and inscription tablature stand out visually as a single unit. The illusion is of a monument within a monument (Fig. 43).

The carver's willow consists of a double-lined narrow trunk with diagonal hatching supporting single-line limbs which arch and fall gracefully to the tree's base under the weight of deeply incised leaf pairs. Always a subordinate motif, the willow appears at various locations on Eclectic Man's stones; on the tympanum it complements the urn; when paired with the coffin at the stone's base or within the inscription, the leaves fall curtain-like in the foreground (Fig. 44).

Fig. 44

Four of the coffins, positioned horizontally and draped with willows, appear prominently on the carver's local work.

Two gravestones exhibit a very simple geometric design at the top; however, its significance is ambiguous. It could be a steeple or a somewhat abstract interpretation of a neoclassical tomb. Capt. Shadrack Terry's marker displays a disk containing a six-point rosette below it.

Fig. 45

It is the 1823 Terry grave marker that reveals the carver's most unusual design. Centered at the base of the stone is a shallowly incised, two-masted ship complete with rigging and rope ladders fore and aft. To the right is a perched dove facing the ship holding a leafy twig in its beak, to the left of the ship is a three branch, leafbearing "tree of life" (Fig. 45). None of Eclectic Man's other grave markers carry an epitaph either pictorial or verse. When I first located the upper portion of this stone it was lying almost completely covered in a pasture. My initial assumption upon viewing only the inscription was that the deceased may have seen army service. As a result of this survey, the entire stone was exposed and upon noting the visual epitaph, I now presume Terry was a ship's captain. This gravestone is the only early nineteenth-century pictorial epitaph that I have found in the county.

On another stone fragment (Norwood, 1826) only the inscription and pedestal portion of the tympanum design are visible. A pair of unusual "plants" completes the corners. Very fine, hair-like stems with small, deeply cut leaves extend upward then bend under the apparent weight of what may be lightly etched grape clusters (Fig. 46).

Fig. 46

Fig. 47

A multitude of various sized leaves in a variety of forms decorate and fill the stones. Usually hidden among the foliage are novel, abstract "peanut flowers," with some resembling an open-end figure "8" finished off with interior dots and jots to affect a blossom. Among Eclectic Man's multiplicity of designs, this feature could qualify as his trademark (Fig. 47).

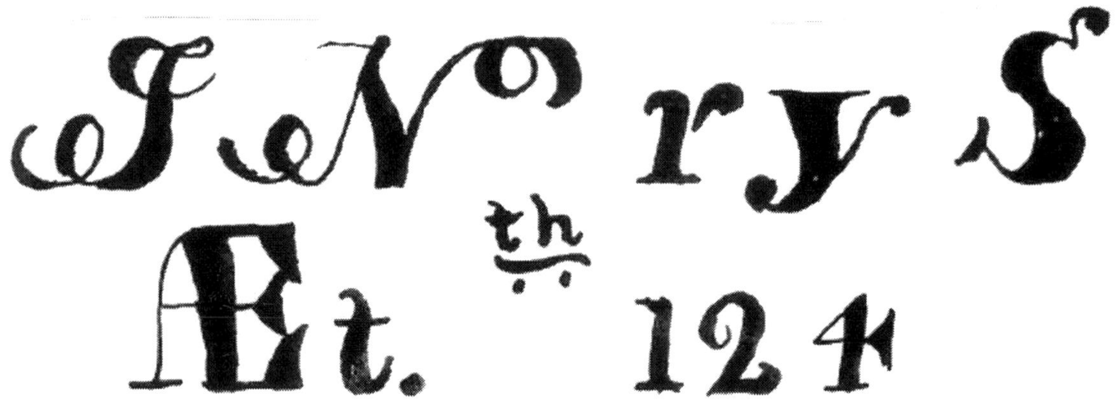

The inscriptions show little consistency except that they all begin with "IN Memory of." The "I" and "N" are large and ornate, at times accented with small hatch marks. On a couple of stones standing in the Old Virgil Cemetery (VL-02), the two letters are widely spaced with foliage between them on one and a willow draped coffin on the other (Fig. 43 & 44). Letters, both linear and cursive, appear in upper and lower case. The styles vary not only from stone to stone but at times within a particular inscription as well. Eclectic Man expanded words and numbers to reach the inscription margins. To accomplish this, he utilized curved line flourishes as fillers and abbreviations formed by deleting vowels and raising end-consonants which he then underlined.

Fig. 48

There are few in-county Eclectic Man stones to work with, yet there is so much to question, especially his relationship to other stone carvers working in the area such as Coffin Man. What was his background prior to arriving in New York's Southern Tier that invested him with his eclectic approach to gravestone carving? A few other gravestones by this carver have been found outside Cortland County. As in Cortland, they are usually single examples, appearing in the towns of Lisle, Richford, Caroline and Dryden, in the counties to the south and west. Farther north there are three more monuments in the Cayuga County community of Venice Center. It is here that a winged angel trumpets over a mounded grave on the 1825 monument for Christiana Harris (Fig. 48).[4]

There isn't a clue thus far to suggest who this stone carver was, where he lived, or what his origins were. His carving expresses the technical skills the craft required but often the quality seems sublimated by his desire to create images in a quantity, or at a pace, that outran his cutting capacity or design abilities. Although his designs appear “busy”, Eclectic Man's craftsmanship reveals both rich diversity and a creative imagination which produced a visual repertoire that is at once curious and exciting.

Endnotes

[1] Virgil Rural Cemetery (VL-01), (l) stone; Old Presbyterian Site (VL-02), (3) stones; Willow Crossing Cemetery (HA-03), (l) stone; Gerrard Cemetery (MA-06), (l) stone; 77 Greenbush St., Cortland, N.Y. (CT-x), (l) stone.

[2] An obituary appears in the *Cortland Repository* March 16, 1816 published at Cortland Village. It reports that Mrs. Sally, wife of Spencer Crary died "in this village" on February 16, 1816. The village burying ground, east of Church Street, was moved in the 1850s to the new Cortland Rural Cemetery when the land was needed for a state teacher's training school. No definitive procedural report or record of removals had been found. In the years since, the school burned and relocated and the site was taken up with the construction of a county courthouse in the early twentieth century. There have been rumors of graves and stones being found over the intervening years. The present location of the Crary grave marker was, until about 1920, known as "Randall Flats" and totally undeveloped. "Fill" had been deposited over the years in that area and since it is only two blocks from the courthouse site excess excavation material may have been disposed of there. The Crary marker, one other inscribed stone and several small footstones or field markers were unearthed while excavating for a house addition.

[3] The Church Book of Virgil compiled by John Sheerar of Cincinnatus [n.d.] contains information abstracted from various Virgil Church records and related materials (on file at the Cortland County Historical Society.) Among the Presbyterian Church records is information that the weekday church meetings were often held at the home of John E. Roe, that he died "during an epidemic" in the spring of 1813 as did two other church members, and in 1823 "the first lettered stone in the cemetery" was placed on the James E. Roe grave.

[4] At Venice Center, Cayuga County there are currently three of Eclectic Man's stones. Ten years ago, Ruth Cummins, a Cortland resident whose many interests include gravestone rubbing, visited that site, noted the trumpeting angel on the tympanum of the Christiana Harris (1825) gravestone and produced a rubbing. She called her work to my attention as I engaged in my stone carver survey. Upon classifying the stone as Eclectic Man's work, I went to Venice Center only to discover that this particular stone is no longer there.

CONCLUSION

What began as a suitable Bicentennial project has grown into a full-fledged obsession. Years ago, as I wound my way throughout Cortland County searching for and wandering about the graveyards, I viewed stones, designs, and images that I felt sure had not really been looked at in many, many years. In retrospect I laugh at my romantic naiveté and burgeoning smugness as I realize that even I, during those first visits, was not truly "seeing."

It was years later, after countless sojourns, that I became aware of patterns emerging--the distinct cutting styles of many stone carvers began to sink into my consciousness. I have learned much about these stones, but I never go back into any of these cemeteries and see only what I saw before. Every visit opens new doors and raises new questions. Some tentative answers to some of my original questions are found within this paper; other puzzles, some old and some new, remain unsolved.

I have taken an initial look at the work of five of the stone carvers whose gravestones stand in Cortland County burial sites bearing dates between 1795 and 1830. (Appendix H) A sparse population and lack of a stable economy for twenty years is reflected in the lack of carved gravestones during that period. Sunburst Man, Coffin Man and Furn Man began to produce tombstones shortly after the county was legally established. Within a few years, as the economy improved and the population increased, the number of gravestones rose as carvers filled orders for both current needs and backdated stones to replace early temporary markers.

Like the early inhabitants, it appears most likely that the early carvers were also native New Englanders. The skilled execution and high quality of their craftsmanship implies that each was a mature, experienced, craftsperson rather than a local novice learning the trade. All except Sunburst Man were itinerant, operating both within and without Cortland County throughout their individual production periods. The lack of a complete inventory for each carver makes it untimely to speculate whether they were exclusively stone carvers or practiced another trade. Additionally, except for Sunburst Man, none of the carvers' work reflects a concentrated production area large enough to recommend local residence.

There is no evidence to suggest that patrons, individually or as a community, expressed a preference in gravestone design. It can be said, after viewing the basic design uniformity and format of each cutter, that each had his own personal style, he cut what he cut and the patron got what he cut. A possible exception to this might be Eclectic Man - customer preference and input may account for his eclecticism.

Cortland's burial sites display no pattern of preference for a particular stone carver. Each site represents the work of the carver, or carvers, who happened to be working in a given area at a given time. There are numerous instances of two or more carvers producing gravestones for various members of one family. The dates reflect the stone carver who was available and working in the area at the time.

As in New England, explicit religious symbolism is absent within the gravestone iconography of Cortland stones. It is only within the epitaphs and aphorisms that there appear any expressions of the perceived relationship with a deity, expectations of salvation, or belief and hope in an afterlife. This deliberate omission in the early nineteenth century would seem to reflect more of a tradition within gravestone designs rather than a continued direct "Puritan" iconophobia, which is theorized by some to have been the prevailing influence for the earliest American gravestones (Ludwig, Tashjian).

The iconographic motifs and inscriptive verses vividly demonstrate the transitional period in gravestone art as the folk icons gave way to popular icons. There exists among these pre-1830 grave markers a wonderful and exciting convergence of themes and styles that successfully blend certain aspects of the initial phase of gravestone art and some eighteenth-century, second-phase vernacular traditions with the nineteenth-century neoclassical motifs.

This generation of gravestone cutters ceased producing gravestones in Cortland County just prior to 1830. Furn Man, Comma Man and Eclectic Man have stones dated 1828 but none later in the county. The tradition ends abruptly. My hypothesis, to explain the cessation at that particular time, is tied to the opening of the Erie Canal in 1825. Within a very few years the entire economic, social and cultural structure of the state changed radically. It was a boom time that brought a flood of people, ideas, and materials across New York State. The machine age and commercialism literally rode the canal packet boats and barges westward. Cortland County felt the impact and was inundated by the overflow.

A tangible manifestation in gravestone art throughout the neoclassical period was the preference for white marble. Quarried in blocks, its design variations were not restricted to the tabular form, although earliest marble tombstones retained that traditional shape for many years.

Just prior to the start of the nineteenth century, the forms commenced to break from the pattern and multi-dimensional configurations provided an almost unlimited number of marble-form variations on which to inscribe memorial inscriptions. Cortland County has many such monuments that were imported from eastern New York, Vermont and elsewhere, engraved locally and erected prior to 1855. There is at least one marble marker in nearly every burial site with more than two marked graves. (Appendix D)

As I discussed in the introduction, there is more to this story. I have not spoken directly at the post-1830 sandstone carvers. Although not as creative nor as rich in iconography as the carvers previously discussed, their work is based on personalized inscriptive engraving. As the last representatives of the local engraving tradition, these craftsmen and their work are also worth documentation and investigation within the scope of this survey, but an in-depth discussion would exceed the parameters of this exercise. I will leave the detail for another essay and briefly comment on the three predominant stone carvers whose work can be seen throughout the length and breadth of Cortland County.

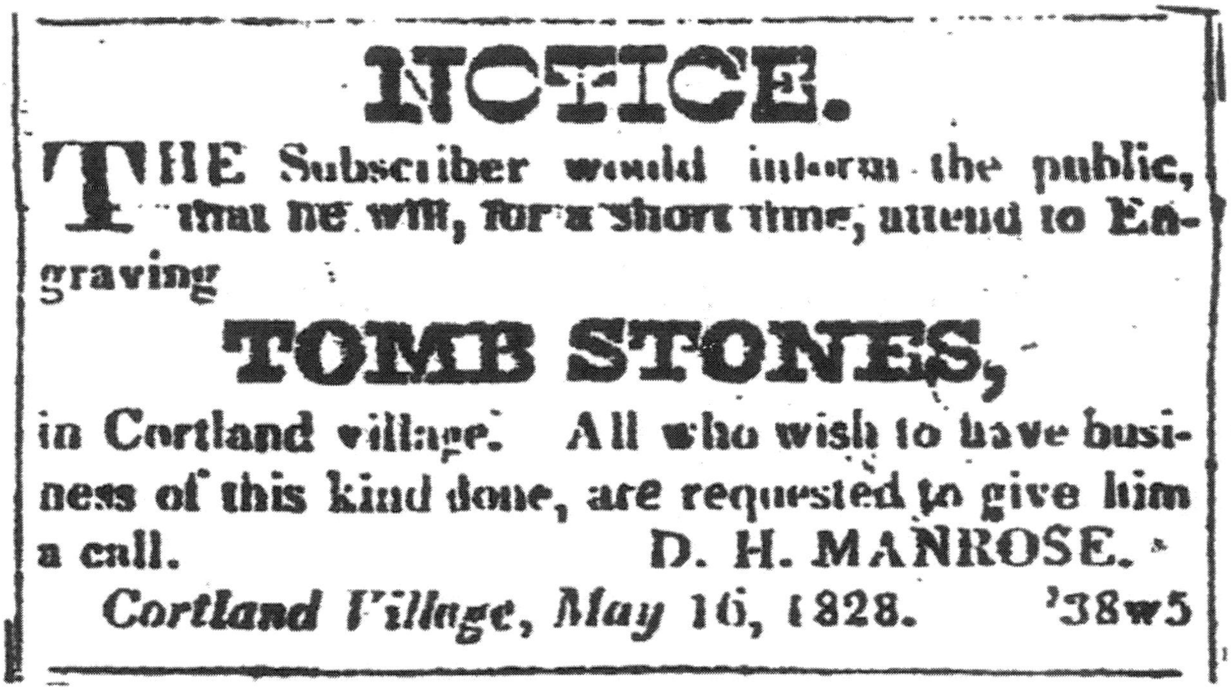
NOTICE.

THE Subscriber would inform the public, that he will, for a short time, attend to Engraving

TOMB STONES,

in Cortland village. All who wish to have business of this kind done, are requested to give him a call.

D. H. MANROSE.

Cortland Village, May 16, 1828. '38w5

Fig. 49 [adapt. From Cortland Observer]

The first to utilize the new technology's pre-designed sandstone slots or blanks was David H. Manrose, an early pioneer whose farm stood at Freetown Corners. His advertisement ran in the Cortland Observer during the spring of 1828, the same year the earlier group of carvers ceased to do business locally (Fig. 49). I have not located a signed stone but have assigned a body of work (more than 150 gravestones) to this carver. Many of the stones are among the county's largest, standing 60 inches out of the ground; consistently reddish-brown, fine-grained sandstone displaying slightly curved tops and exhibiting deeply incised, modified-cursive inscriptions. Among Manrose's inventory is a stone for Thomas Russell (1834) whose estate lists $11.50 "paid for tombstone engrav[ing]."[1] Manrose himself died in 1838, not one of this distinct group of gravestones is dated after 1836.

Asa Joiner, on the contrary, signed at least fifteen of the nearly 600 grave markers which I believe he inscribed over a twenty-year span. His work, on a variety of reddish-brown sandstone textures and sizes bears an overall resemblance to Manrose work; however, they were very diverse when it came to certain letters and numbers. There is a subgroup of stones within Joiner's inventory which I have designated "Joiner-like-Manrose," most dated between 1828 and 1837. Joiner may have learned to carve inscriptions from Manrose and worked with him in a shop.

The subgroup inventory increases as Manrose's work decreases prior to his death. Joiner was a copier rather than an innovator. He later incorporated the lettering style of his 1840s competitor, P. P. Moore. The 1850 Census lists Joiner as a "stonecutter" when he, his wife Roxann and their four children, were living in the Town of Harford. The residence was in Babcock Hollow, not far from Virgil. Ironically, my records indicate he produced only one stone that year, within a short time Asa Joiner left Cortland County.

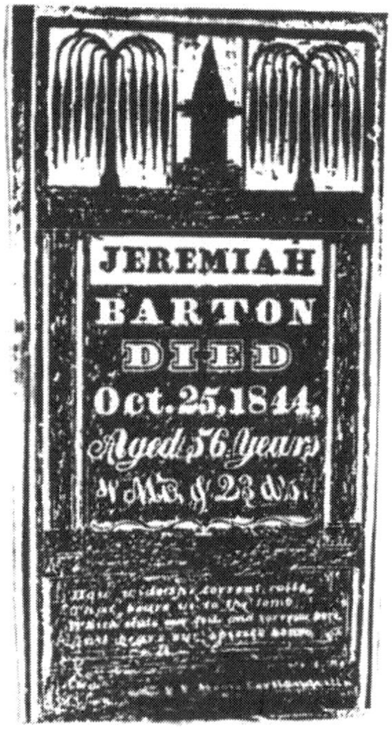

Fig. 50

Philo Perry Moore was an early resident of the Town of Virgil. He later set up shop in the Village of Cortland where he worked in both sandstone and marble, unlike the two previous mentioned carvers. The 1850 Census lists both he and his brother, Hiram, as sculptors. P. P. Moore's style is all his own. Each line of the inscription is artfully and meticulously cut in a different lettering style, one in relief (usually the given name) and the others elegantly incised (Fig. 50). He signed several of the nearly 200 tombstones engraved between the late 1830s and 1854. (Appendix I)

Sandstone monuments virtually "die" in the graveyards of Cortland County by 1855. Only a handful can be found with a later date. White marble glistens in the sunlight: the neoclassical influence in gravestone art, artists and material consumed the earlier traditions. The machine age brought a new technology, new ideas and a new wealth and prosperity to a young country rapidly expanding on all frontiers.

The folk imagination is one that thrives in restricted pockets of culture. Cortland's relative geographic isolation prior to the canal opening, coupled with its predominantly rural construct, produced positive factors which supported and encouraged early-migrating, traditional stone carvers to continue creating their inspired, vernacular imagery. As in New England's sculptured designs, "rural stone carving was marked by a concern for line, a propensity toward geometric effects and an interest in stylized clarity" (Ludwig 428).

Competent, skilled engravers, their artistic talents now grace my native county with striking, often provocative examples of gravestone art. Their legacy in stone elicits both an appreciation of their work and a sense of curiosity and intrigue with regard to their identity and origins. Though many scholars focus on the New England "faces" and imply that these images alone are the only motifs worthy of serious study, documentation and praise, I do not agree. The theory of uninspired urn and willow is not supported by the artifacts found in Cortland County produced by the carvers presented here and others whose work is still to be documented. Within Cortland County's burial sites, I believe that there is ample evidence of originality and creativity to claim that American gravestone sculpture, strongly reflective of rural stone carving traditions, did exist outside New England in the nineteenth century.

Endnotes

[1] The information concerning payment for "tombstone engrav[ing] $11. 50" was found in Probate File X9510 - Estate of Thomas Russell, "Affidavit & Settlement" form, filed 6 June 1836, Cortland County Surrogate Record Room, Courthouse, Cortland, N.Y. Thomas Russell died April 23, 1834 and he is buried in the Old Virgil (Presbyterian) Cemetery (VL-02).

Of the 513 survey cards completed for this project, the 246 adults were selected and crosschecked with the Testate and Intestate indices for estate settlements. This produced thirty-five files, only two of which were for females. The contents of each was investigated. The Russell comment is the only reference to a gravestone discovered to-date. There was no receipt for payment in the folder; therefore, the identity of the engraver remains unknown for certain, but the inscription on the stone in question belongs to the body of work I have tentatively assigned to David H. Manrose of Freetown Corners.

Bibliography

Bain, George. Celtic Art: The Methods of Construction. New York: Dover Publications, Inc., 1973.

Benes, Peter J. The Masks of Orthodoxy: Folk Gravestone Carving in Plymouth County, Massachusetts, 1689-1805. Amherst: University of Massachusetts Press, 1977.

Buckeye, Nancy. "Early American Gravestone Studies: The Structure of the Literature" and "Bibliography of Gravestone Art." Puritan Gravestone Art. Ed. Peter Benes. The Dublin Seminar for New England Folklife, Annual Proceedings, 1976. Boston: Boston University, 1977. 130-141.

Caulfield, Ernest. "Wanted: The Hook-and-Eye Man." Markers. Worcester: AGS Publications, 1980. 15-47.

Census For 1820. Washington: Gales and Seaton, 1821, p. 10.

Coats, Donald R. "General Geology of South Central New York." State Geology Association, 35th Annual Meeting at Binghamton, N.Y., 1963.

Combs, Diana Williams. Early Gravestone Art in Georgia and South Carolina. Athens, Ga.: The University of George Press, 1986.

Cortland Observer. 30 May 1828, p. 1, col. 1. Cortland Free Library, Cortland, N. Y.

Deetz, James. In Small Things Forgotten: The Archeology of Early American Life. Garden City, N.Y.: Anchor Press/Doubleday, 1977.

Dethlefsen, E. and James Deetz. "Deaths' Heads, Cherubs, and Willow Trees: Experimental Archeology in Colonial Cemeteries." American Antiquity 31 (1966): 502-510.

Duval, Francis Y. and Ivan Rigsby. Early American Gravestone Art in Photographs. New York: Dover Publications, 1978.

Dwight, Timothy. Travels in New England and New York. Vol. IV. Cambridge: The Belknap Press of Harvard University Press, 1969.

Ellis, David M. et al. History of New York State. Ithaca: Cornell University Press, 1967.

Forbes, Harriette Merrifield. Gravestones of Early New England and the Men Who Made Them: 1653-1800. New York: DaCapo Press, 1967.

French, J. H. Gazetteer of the State of New York. Syracuse: R. Pearsall Smith, 1860. 250-256.

George, Diana Hume and Malcolm A. Nelson. "Resurrecting the Epitaph." Markers. Worcester: AGS Publications, 1980. 85-95.

Gillon, Edmund Vincent, Jr. Early New England Gravestone Rubbings. New York: Dover Publications, 1966.

Glassie, Henry. "Artifacts: Folk, Popular, Imaginary and Real." Icons of Popular Culture. Ed. Marshall Fishwick and Ray B. Browne. Bowling Green: University Press, 1970.

Glassie, Henry Pattern in the Material Folk Culture of the Eastern United States. Philadelphia: University of Pennsylvania Press, 1968.

Heads of Families at the First Census of the United States Taken in the Year 1790. Vol. I, Maine. Vol. II, New Hampshire. Vol. III, Vermont. Vol. IV, Massachusetts. Vol. V, Rhode Island. Vol. VI, Connecticut. Vol. VII, New York. Washington: Government Printing Office, 1908.

Heaslip, W. Graham. "Paleontology and Stratigraphy of the Cortland-Syracuse- Ithaca Area." Fieldtrip Guidebook Cortland Area. Cortland: SUNY Cortland, 1966. 16-24.

Ludwig, Allan I. Graven Images: New England Stonecarving and Its Symbols, 1650-1815. Middletown, Ct.: Wesleyan University Press, 1966.

Markers. The Annual Journal of the Association for Gravestone Studies. Vol. I. Ed. Jessie L. Farber. Worcester: AGS Publications, 1980.

Markers II. The Journal of the Association for Gravestone Studies. Ed. David Watters. Lanham, Md.: University Press of America, 1983.

Markers III. The Journal of the Association for Gravestone Studies. Ed. David Watters. Lanham, Md.: University Press of America, 1985.

Matthias, George F. "Weathering Rates of Portland Arkose Tombstones" The Journal of Geological Education 15 (1967): 140-144.

"Meet the Residents of Keeney Settlement" [transcript] Cuyler Historical Society, Cuyler, N. Y., 1980.

Muller, Ernest H. "Glacial and Geomorphology Between Cortland and Syracuse." Fieldtrip Guidebook Cortland Area. Cortland: SUNY Cortland, 1966. 2-6.

Pattern in the Material Folk Culture of the Eastern United States. Philadelphia: University of Pennsylvania, 1968.

Perley, Sidney. "Early Gravestones in Essex County." in Essex Antiquarian 3:12, December 1899: 177-181.

Puritan Gravestone Art. Proceedings of the Dublin Seminar for New England Folklife, 1976. Vol. I. Dublin, N. H.: Boston University and Dublin Seminar for New England Folklife, 1980.

"Quarries of Bluestone and Other Sandstones in the Upper Devonian of New York State." New York State Museum. Merrill, Frederick J. H., Dir. Bulletin 61, Economic Geology. Albany: University of New York, 1902.

Rahn, Perry H. "The Weathering of Tombstones and Its Relationship to the Topography of New England." The Journal of Geological Education, Vol 19 (1971): 112-118.

Seventh United States Population Census, 1850 County of Cortland, New York. Office of the County Clerk, Courthouse, Cortland, N.Y.

Stannard, David E. The Puritan Way of Death. New York: Oxford University Press, 1977.

Stokes, Margaret Ruth Little. "Sticks and Stones: A Profile of North Carolina Grave markers Through Three Centuries." Dissertation, University of North Carolina at Chapel Hill, 1984.

Tashjian, Dickran and Anne Tashjian. Memorials For Children of Change. Middletown, Ct.: Wesleyan University Press, 1974.

Trask, Deborah E. Life How Short, Eternity How Long: Gravestone Carving and Carvers in Nova Scotia. Halifax, N. S.: Nova Scotia Museum, 1978.

Wasserman, Emily. Gravestone Designs: Rubbings and Photographs From Early New York and New Jersey. New York: Dover Publications, Inc., 1972.

Welch, Richard F. The Gravestones of Early Long Island, 1680-1810. Syosset, N. Y.: Friends for Long Island's Heritage, 1983.

Willsher, Betty and Doreen Hunter. Stones: A Guide To Some Remarkable Eighteenth-Century Gravestones. New York: Taplinger Publishing Co., 1979.

MAP OF TOWNS - CORTLAND COUNTY, NEW YORK

With Cemetery Locations

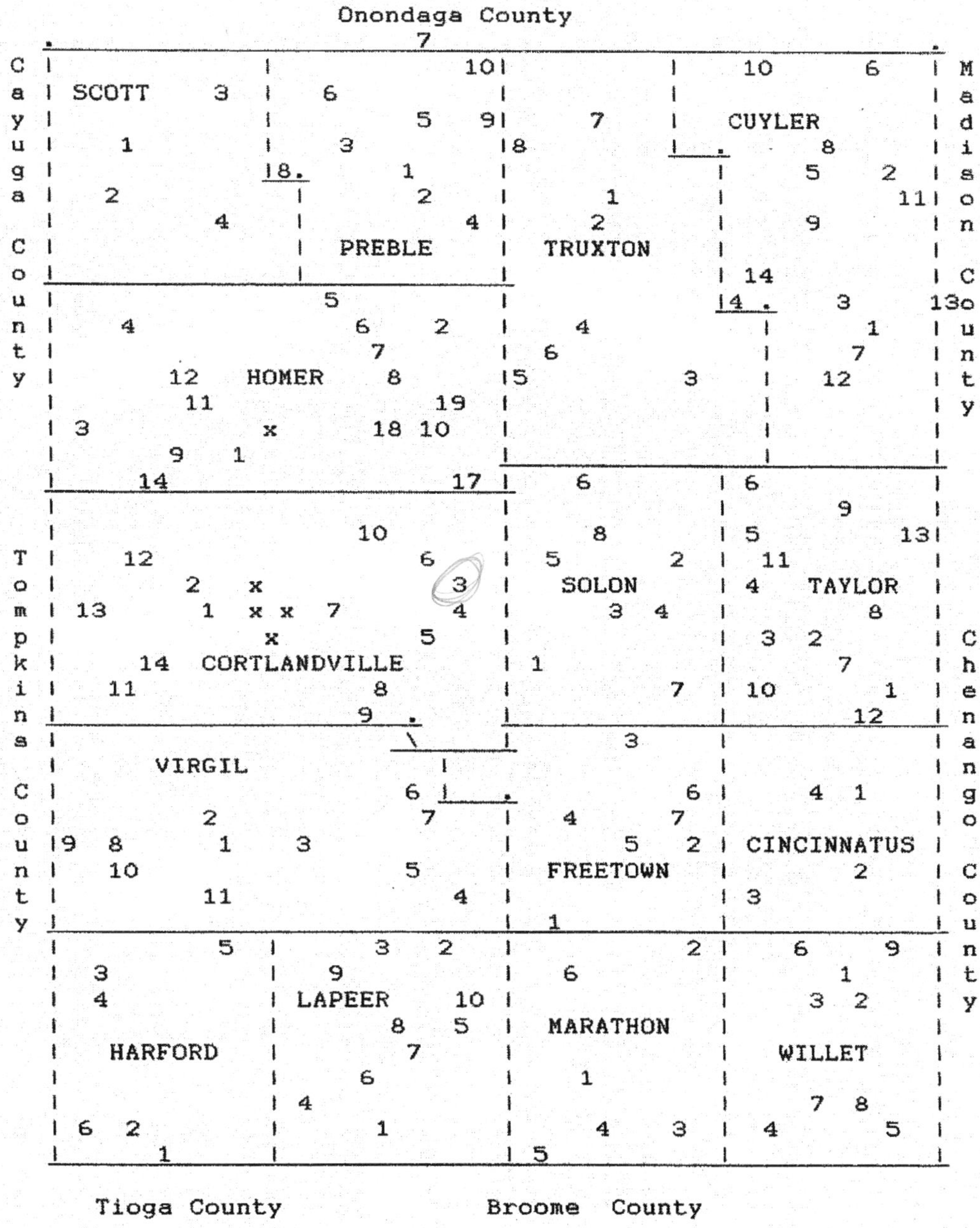

MAP OF TOWNS - CORTLAND COUNTY, NEW YORK

With Cemetery Locations *

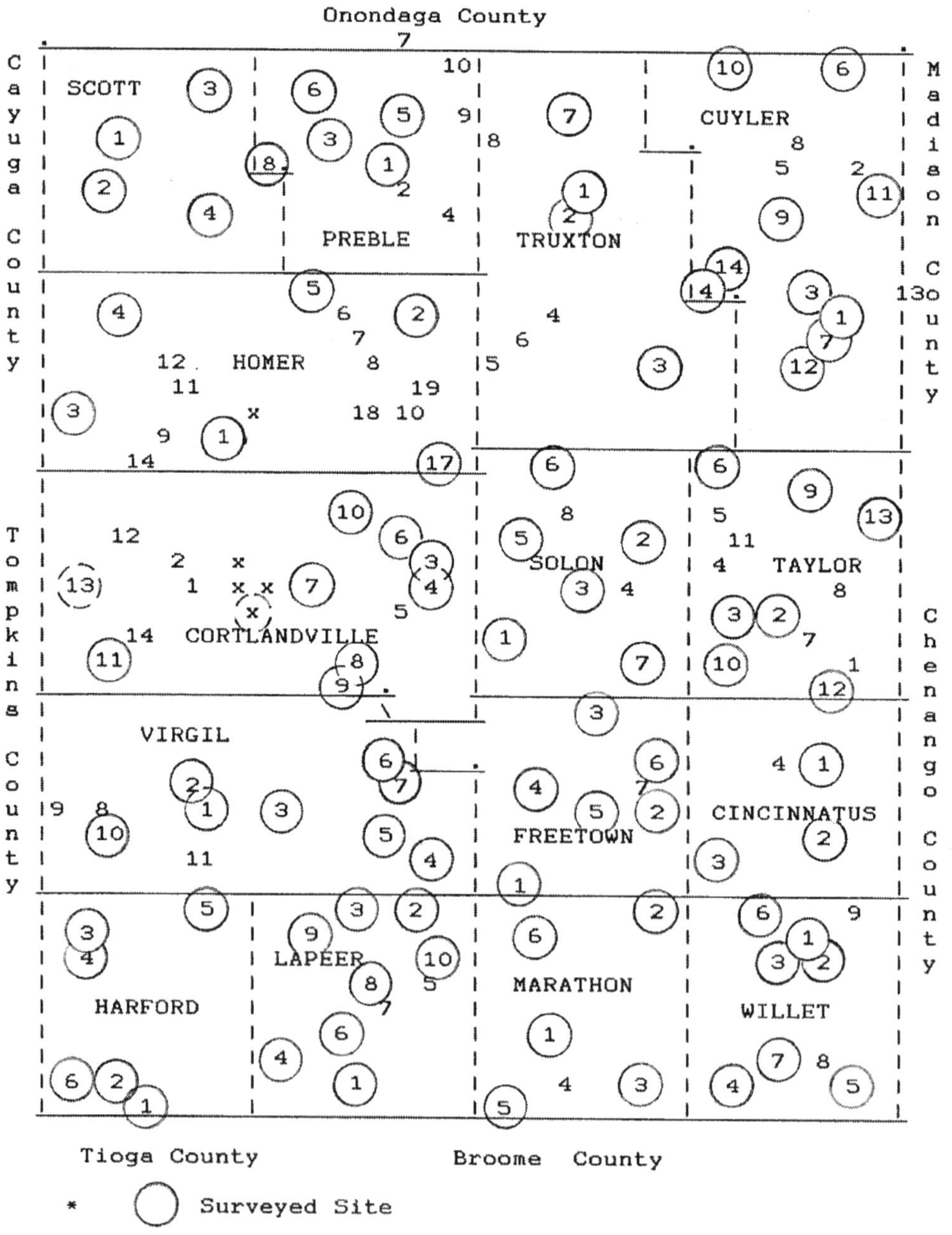

CORTLAND COUNTY, N.Y. BURIAL SITES VISITED

For the Purpose of Gathering Information
Re: Gravestone Carver Survey Project: 1985-1986

Town	Site #	Site	Status
Cincinnatus (CN)	01	Village Cemetery	C
	02	Lower Village Site	C
	03	Dutch Hill Site	A
Cortlandville (CT)	03	McGraw Rural Cemetery	C
	04	Old Baptist Site (McGraw)	A
	06	Hicks Vault	A
	07	Conable Farm Cemetery	T
	08	Blodgett Mills (old)	T
	09	Forest Home Cemetery	C
	10	County Farm Cemetery	T
	11	South Cortland Cemetery	T
	13	Sears Rd	(site gone – 2 stones)
	x	77 Greenbush Street, Cortland	
Cuyler (CU)	01	Seventh Day Baptist	T
	03	Muncy Hill Site	T
	04	Winnie Family Site	A
	06	Cowles Settlement	A
	07	Cuyler Hill Site	A
	09	Cuyler Village Cemetery	C
	10	Keeney Settlement Cemetery	C
	11	Madison County Line Site	A
	12	Abraham Hollenbeck Site	A
	14	Hoyer Cemetery	A
Freetown (FR)	01	Galatia Cemetery	T
	02	Gardiner Cemetery	A
	03	Underwood Cemetery	A
	04	Freetown Corners	C
	05	Wilbur Farm Site	A
	06	Fox Road Cemetery	A
Harford (HA)	01	Harford Mills Cemetery	C
	02	Harford Village Cemetery	C
	03	Willow Crossing Site	A

Town	Site #	Site	Status
Harford (HA)	04	Cotterill Road Site	T
	05	Tillotson Farm Site	A
	06	Slaterville Road Site	T
Homer (HO)	01	Glenwood Cemetery	C
	02	East Homer Cemetery	C
	03	West Homer Cemetery	C
	04	Atwater Cemetery	C
	05	Little York Cemetery	T
	17a	Phelps Road	A
Lapeer (LA)	01	Hunts Corners Cemetery	T?
	02	Price/Ayers Site	T
	03	Parker Street Cemetery	C
	04	Clarks Corners Cemetery	T
	06	Quail Hill/Parker Site	A?
	08	Highland Road Cemetery	T
	09	Quail Hollow Site	A
	10	Muckey Road Site	A
Marathon (MA)	01	Marathon Rural Cemetery	C
	02	Texas Valley Cemetery	C
	03	Merrill Creek Road Site	A
	05	Tim Hill Road Site (Bemis)	T
	06	Gerrard Family Site	A
Preble (PR)	01	Elmwood Cemetery	C
	03	Town Garage Site	T
	05	Old Presbyterian Site (Currie Road)	T
	06	Masters Cemetery	T
	08	Mt. Toppin Cemetery	A
Scott (SC)	01	Seventh Day Baptist	T
	02	Scott Union Cemetery	C
	03	Underwood/Ames Cemetery	T
	04	Gillette Cemetery	T
Solon (SO)	01	Greenman Cemetery	T
	02	Maplewood Cemetery	T?
	03	Baptist Church Cemetery	T?
	05	Bingham Cemetery (Lapp Road)	A
	06	Chapin Family Cemetery	A
	07	East Freetown Cemetery	A

Town	Site #	Site	Status
Taylor (TA)	02	Bush Family Site	T
	03	Hawley Cemetery	A
	06	Gay Family Site	T
	09	Potter Hill Cemetery	T
	10	Phelps Family Cemetery	T
	12	Taylor Village Cemetery	C
	13	Union Valley Cemetery	C
Truxton (TX)	01	Truxton Rural Cemetery	C
	02	St. Patrick's Cemetery	C
	03	Cheningo Cemetery	C
	07	Labrador Cemetery	T
Virgil (VL)	01	Virgil Rural Cemetery	C
	02	Old Presbyterian Site (Old Virgil)	T
	03	Seager Cemetery	A
	04	Palmer Family Cemetery	A
	05	Snyder Hill Site	A?
	06	West River Road (Upper)	A
	07	West River Road (Lower)	A
	10	Teeter Road Site	A
Willet (WL)	01	Willet Village Cemetery	C
	02	Burlingame Cemetery	T
	03	Hetty Greene Site	T
	04	Barry Hollow Site	T
	05	Eaton Hill Site	A
	06	Bloody Pond Road Site	T
	07	Site 7	T

Status:

A – Abandoned/Not Maintained
C – Currently Processing Burials/Maintenance Varies
T – Town Responsible for Maintenance/Care Varies

APPENDIX D

PRE – 1855 GRAVE MARKERS

SITES SURVEYED		TYPE & QUANTITY			
Town	**Site #**	**Fieldstone**	**Sandstone**	**Marble**	**Total**
Cincinnatus (CN)	01	3	54	72	129 +/-
	02		16	35	51
	03	5	1	2	8
Cortlandville (CT)	03		13	NC	?
	04		25	41	66
	06		-	1	1
	07	5	26	8	39
	08	5	23	3	31
	09		2	-	2
	10		22	9	31+
	11	4	26	3	33
	13		2	-	2
	x		2	-	2
Cuyler (CU)	01		1	6	7*
	03		1	7	8*
	04		6	4	10
	06		-	2	2
	07		7	3	10*
	09	6	23	25	54
	10		27	51	78
	11		1	1	2*
	12		1	-	1*
	14		4	1	5
Freetown (FR)	01	10	16	3	29
	02		-	3	3*
	03	2	3	1	6
	04		29	19	48
	05		2	-	2*
	06		1	1	2*

SITES SURVEYED		TYPE & QUANTITY			
Town	**Site #**	**Fieldstone**	**Sandstone**	**Marble**	**Total**
Harford (HA)	01		44	27	71
	02		1	NC	?*
	03	2	1	-	3
	04	5	4	6	15
	05		3	-	3
	06	8	3	7	18
Homer (HO)	01		29	120+	149+
	02	4	25	18	47
	03	1	16	11+	28+
	04		33	46+	79+
	05	10	13	9	32
	17a		-	1	1
Lapeer (LA)	01	3	21	5	29
	02	1	3	-	4*
	03	1	7	14	22
	04		8	4	12
	06		6	1	7
	08		14	2	16
	09	2	3	-	5
	10		2	-	2*
Marathon (MA)	01		13	158+/-	171+/-
	02	2	63	23	88
	03		9	5	14
	05	4	23	12	39
	06	3+	4	5	12+
Preble (PR)	01		4	45+	49+
	03		3	2	5
	05		20	5	25
	06	6	-	4	10
	08	8+/-	7+	2	17+/-
Scott (SC)	01	2	44	72	118
	02		-	4	4*
	03		4	1	5
	04		11	5	16

SITES SURVEYED		TYPE & QUANTITY			
Town	**Site #**	**Fieldstone**	**Sandstone**	**Marble**	**Total**
Solon (SO)	01	23+/-	11	4	38+/-
	02		-	4	4
	03	10	3	11	24
	05	2	9	1	12
	06	11	7	6	24
	07		8	14	22
Taylor (TA)	02	10	3	12	25
	03		-	3	3*
	06	4	2	5	11*
	09		6	38	44
	10	1	5	18	24
	11		-	1	1
	12		1	NC	?
	13		17	26	43
Truxton (TX)	01		66	22	88
	02		-	2	2
	03	8	27	16	51
	07	8	29	6	43
Virgil (VL)	01	1	49	29+	79+
	02		39	23+	62+
	03	7	20+	3+	30+
	04		4	-	4
	05	3	26	14	43
	06		2	1	3*
	07		2	-	2
	10		4	-	4
Willet (WL)	01		6	50+	56+
	02	10	9	1	20
	03		6	3	9
	04	16	4	2	22
	05		1	-	1
	06		-	1	1
	07		2	-	2*
TOTALS		**216+**	**1143+**	**1231+**	**2590+**

(*) - Stone type counted - full Site Inventory not done.
(NC) - Not counted due to high number of marble stones randomly scattered over a large site.
(+) - Count believed short due to poor condition/illegibility of some markers.
(+/-) – Count variable due to questionable dates and deteriorated condition of grave markers.

Surveyed Sites Contiguous to Cortland County

ONONDAGA COUNTY
Cold Brook Cemetery
South Spafford Cemetery
Howard Family Cemetery
(Otisco Rd. at Fuller)
Pine Ridge Cemetery (Navarino)
Site at Route 80 & Octagon Road
Vesper Cemetery
Tully Cemetery
Fabius Cemetery
Apulia Cemetery
Delphi Falls Cemetery
VanBergen Cemetery
Cardiff Cemetery
Amber Cemetery

CAYUGA COUNTY
Genoa Cemetery (Rt. 90)
East Genoa (Rt. 38)
Venice Center Cemetery
Venice Baptist Church Cemetery

TOMPKINS COUNTY
Dryden Old Cemetery
Etna Cemetery
Caroline Grove Cemetery
Barnyard Site off Gee Hill Road

TIOGA COUNTY
Richford at Congregational Church
Newark Valley – Route 38
Newark Valley - 1 mile south on Rte. 38

BROOME COUNTY
Upper Lisle Cemetery
Lisle Cemetery
Killawog Cemetery
Whitney Point Cemetery
Barker Site on Route 11

MADISON COUNTY
DeRuyter Old Cemetery
South Otselic Cemetery

CHENANGO COUNTY
Ufford Cemetery
Hinman Cemetery
Pitcher Cemetery
Schoolhouse Site at County Line
Smithville Flats
Bainbridge
West Bainbridge
Coventryville
Bennettsville

DELAWARE COUNTY
Downsville (Covered Bridge Site)
Masonville Cemetery

SURVEY CARD

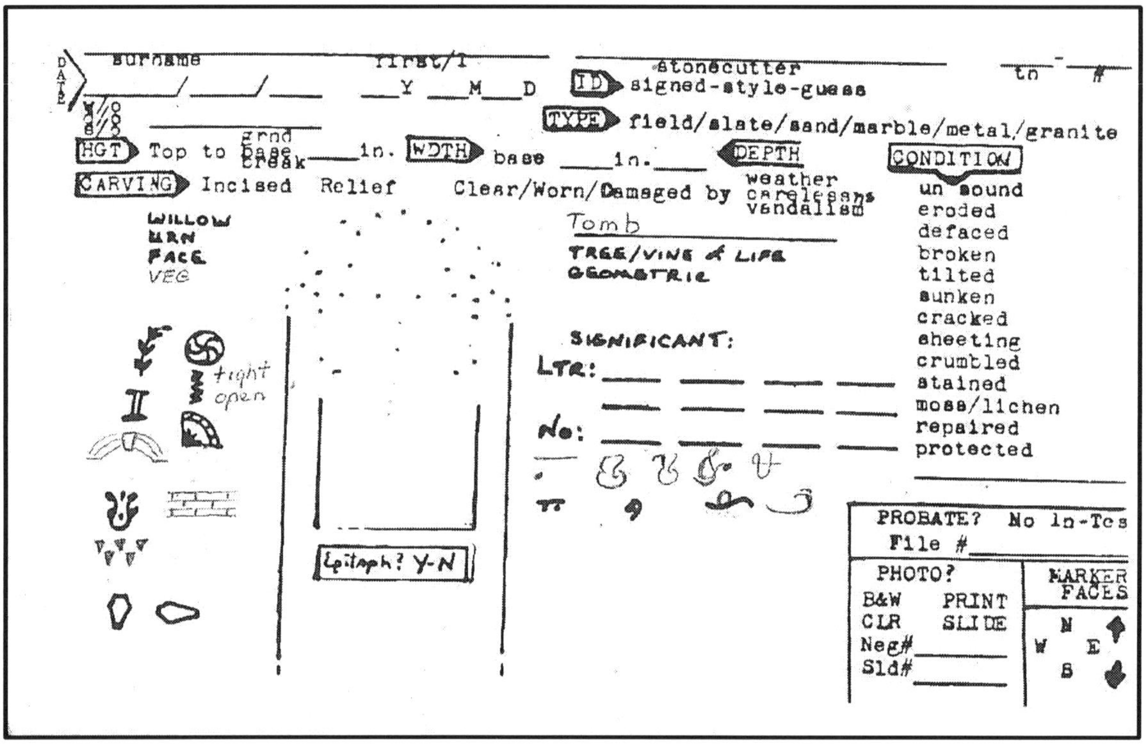
DATE
surname
first/I
Y M D
stonecutter
ID signed-style-guess
tn #
W/O
S/O
TYPE field/slate/sand/marble/metal/granite
HGT Top to grnd base break in.
WDTH base in.
DEPTH
CONDITION
CARVING Incised Relief
Clear/Worn/Damaged by weather carelessns vandalism
un sound
eroded
defaced
broken
tilted
sunken
cracked
sheeting
crumbled
stained
moss/lichen
repaired
protected
WILLOW
URN
FACE
VEG
Tomb
TREE/VINE of LIFE
GEOMETRIC
tight
open
SIGNIFICANT:
LTR:
No:
Epitaph? Y-N
PROBATE? No In-Tcs
File #
PHOTO?
B&W PRINT
CLR SLIDE
Neg#
Sld#
MARKER FACES
N
W E
S

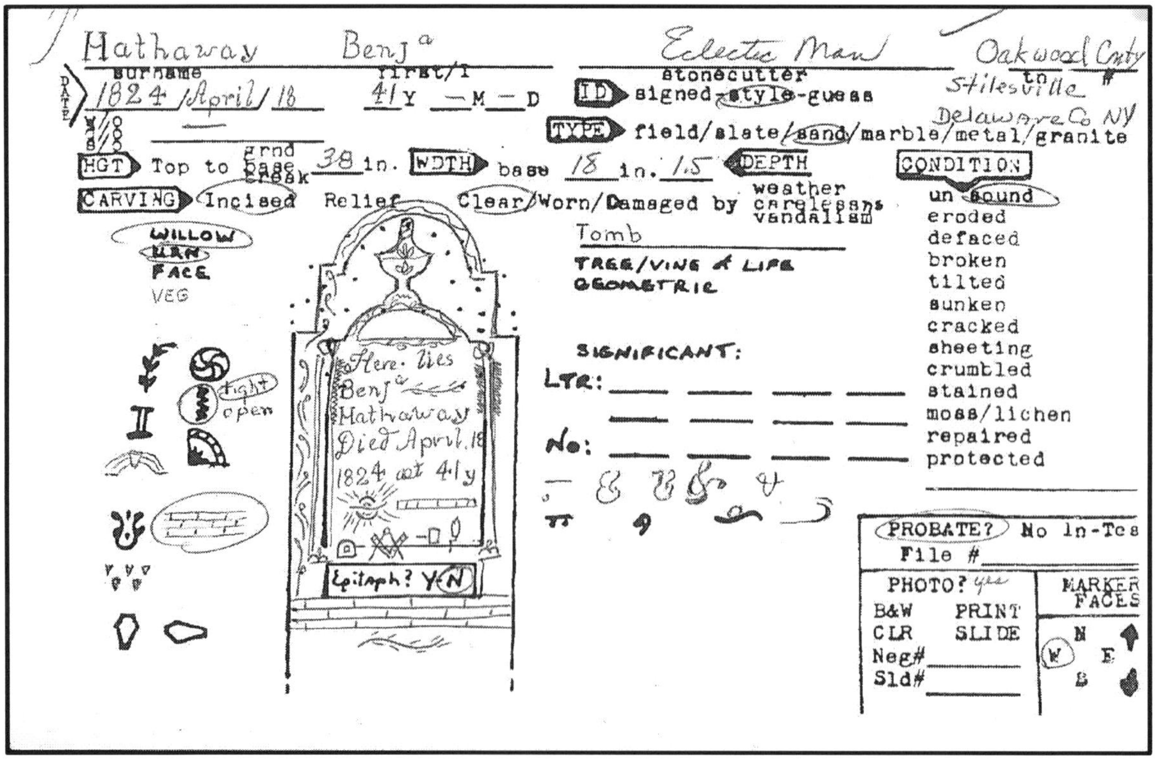
Hathaway
Benj a
surname
first/I
1824 April 18
41 Y M D
Eclectic Man
stonecutter
ID signed-style-guess
Oakwood Cmty
Stilesville
Delaware Co NY
tn #
W/O
S/O
TYPE field/slate/sand/marble/metal/granite
HGT Top to grnd base break 38 in.
WDTH base 18 in. 1.5
DEPTH
CONDITION
CARVING Incised Relief
Clear/Worn/Damaged by weather carelessns vandalism
un sound
eroded
defaced
broken
tilted
sunken
cracked
sheeting
crumbled
stained
moss/lichen
repaired
protected
WILLOW
URN
FACE
VEG
Tomb
TREE/VINE of LIFE
GEOMETRIC
Here lies
Benj a
Hathaway
Died April 18
1824 at 41 y
tight
open
SIGNIFICANT:
LTR:
No:
Epitaph? Y-N
PROBATE? No In-Tcs
File #
PHOTO? yes
B&W PRINT
CLR SLIDE
Neg#
Sld#
MARKER FACES
N
W E
S

GRAVESTONE CARVERS WHO PRODUCED TOMBSTONES PRIOR TO 1855 IN CORTLAND COUNTY, NEW YORK

Name/Pseudonym	Date Span	Geographic Area
SUNBURST MAN	1802-1823	N.E. County
COMMA MAN	1816-1828	All county (Chenango, Broome Counties)
F[URN] MAN	1808-1828	All county (Onondaga County)
COFFIN MAN	1811-1820	S.E. County (Chenango, Broome, Delaware Counties)
ECLECTIC MAN	1809-1826	S.W. County (Broome, Tioga, Tompkins, Cayuga Counties)
DAVID H. MANROSE	ca.1820-1835	All county and Adjacent Counties
"J.L. CRANDALL Sculptor"	1812	Truxton 07 (Labrador)
"ASA JOINER - Virgil"	ca. 1827-1850?	All county and Adjacent Counties
"L. PECK-Solon" (Lymon Peck)	1838	Texas Valley Cemetery in Town of Marathon
"P.P. MOORE Cortland V" (Philo Perry Moore)	ca. 1833-1853	North County (Sandstone & Marble)
"P.P. & C.G. MOORE Cortland V"	1845-1849	Towns of Scott & Truxton
HIRAM MOORE	ca. 1850	No signed example found
"C WHITING, JR. Virgil" (Caleb Whiting, Jr.)	ca. 1840-1849	South County (Marble Only)
"R LYON – Homer" (Reuben Lyon)	1852	Town of Homer (Marble Only)
"SWEET & BURCH - Virgil"	1848	Town of Homer (Marble Only)

ca. means circa or about

PRODUCTION COMPARISON - YEAR/QUANTITY

PRE – 1830 SANDSTONE CARVERS
Cortland County, New York

Date	Sunburst	Coffin	Comma	Eclectic	Furn
Unknown	*				*
1799		*			
1800					
1801					
1802	*				
1803	*				
1804					
1805					
1806	*				
1807					
1808				*	**
1809	*				*
1810					***
1811		**			*
1812	**	**			*
1813	*	**		*	******
1814		**			**
1815	*	*			***
1816		******	*	*	*
1817	**	*			**
1818	**	**	*		*
1819		*******			
1820		*	**		***
1821				*	**
1822	*				****
1823	*			*	*******
1824			*	*	
1825			***		****
1826			****	*	*
1827			***		******
1828			***		****
1829					
1830					

POST – 1830 CUTTERS

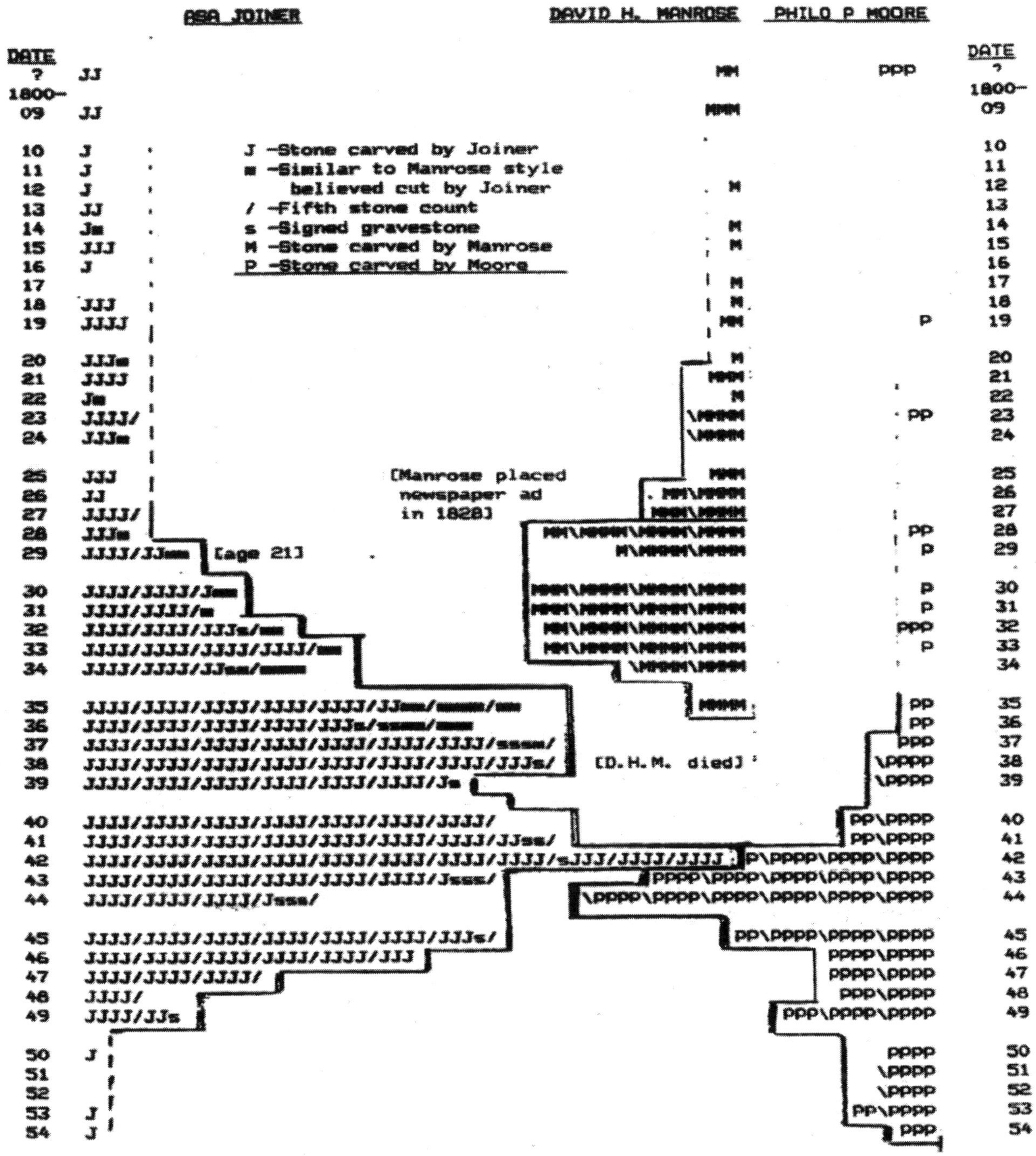

PART TWO

IT ONLY TAKES ONE STONE

The Search for Coffin Man

2006

In 1975, while updating a Bicentennial cemetery survey for Cortland County, I found myself in the Texas Valley Cemetery, tucked into the rural landscape of upstate New York. Attracted to a sandstone grave marker with a large heart in the tympanum, I gazed down and below the inscription I saw two vertical coffins framed by an arching willow. “How odd” I thought and wondered if there were more stones with similar coffins. A search of the cemetery revealed sixteen additional gravestones by the same carver, thirteen bore the upright coffins. His carving design and style were unique in that cemetery. That first summer I found fourteen more of the carver’s stones in nearby burial sites. He had placed the upright coffin icon on six of those markers. The death dates spanned the second decade of the nineteenth century and appeared to be engraved by an experienced craftsman early in the county’s history.[1]

Barto children d. 1819
Texas Valley Cemetery
Cortland Co., NY

These coffin icons so fascinated me that I felt compelled to learn the stone carver’s identity, and through his work place him and his inventory into the historical record of central New York. In the end, my curiosity lured me across four states into hundreds of cemeteries to view thousands of gravestones. The investigation incorporated a kaleidoscope of courthouse records, library resources, archive manuscripts, maps, early newspapers, private collections, and personal contacts. I could never have imagined how long and how far such a quest would carry me. My ever-increasing curiosity about the coffin carver’s identity, his origins, and the odd treasury of images so out of sync with time and place, sustained me as years slipped past. I never dreamed that first single gravestone would engage my attention for twenty years. I learned that identifying this stone carver could depend on finding “*one stone*” coupled with an estate record that would name him. Throughout the intervening years I became absorbed in the search for that other stone which could unravel the puzzle. This odyssey changed my life forever.

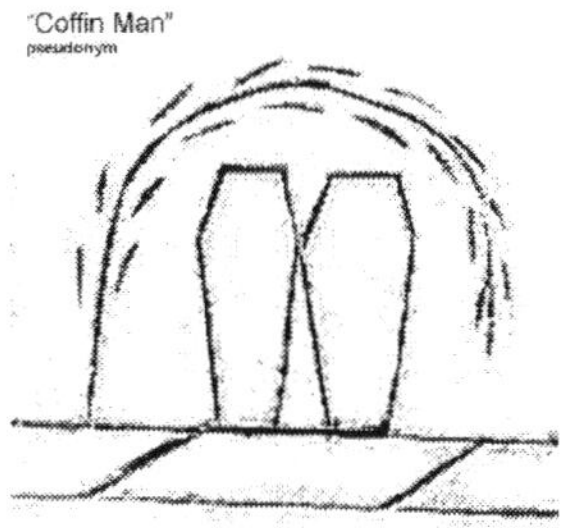

Barto children d. 1819
Texas Valley Cemetery
Cortland Co., NY

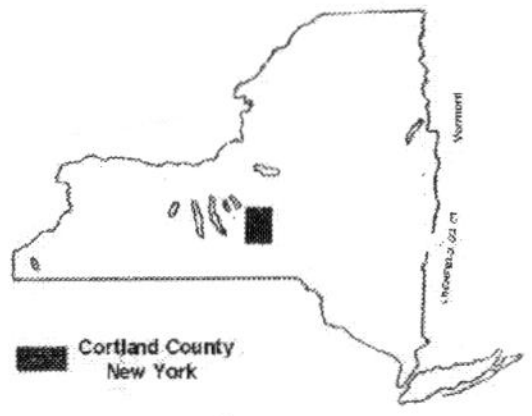

[1] Cortland County established in 1808, previously the southern half of Onondaga County.

Texas Valley is nestled among the rolling green hills in the southeast corner of my native Cortland County, New York. The coffins that had caught my eye were etched below the inscription. A few stones displayed more than one coffin which reflected the multiple names of the dead recorded on the memorial. Initially I attributed seventeen gravestones to the artisan at this location, thirteen displayed the vertical coffin configuration. This carver needed a temporary identity and the pseudonym *"Coffin Man"* came easily.

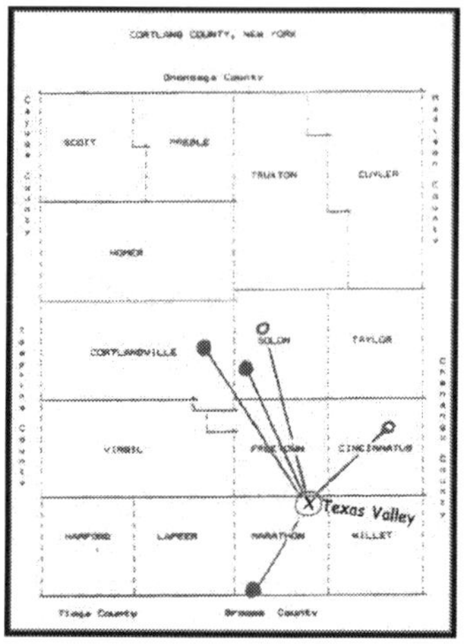

Texas Valley, Cortland Co., NY

Jacob Edick d. 1807
Rev. Soldier Cemetery
Deposit, Broome Co., NY

His gravestone format was simple and clean overall and the ornamentation on each was unique. Fourteen of the memorials were engraved with the obsolete salutary phrase "Here Lies," the balance expressed "In Memory of." Death dates ranged from 1811 through 1819 and the stone he used was consistently gray-brown native sandstone, commonly called greywacke. The surface was unpolished, though it had been dressed off flat enough to produce an acceptable rubbing. With exceptions, the tympanum exhibited the half-round form, set on square shoulders. The size of the stones was generally small with an average height of 30-40 inches out of the ground, average width of 14 inches and an average thickness of 1-2 inches.

The Coffin Man's engraving was well spaced, with design and lettering cut uniformly shallow, and yet the incised edges had not been dulled by time. I marveled that a man could hammer a chisel with such delicate control, letters and numbers appeared as though struck mechanically. He surely used a guideline to carve so precisely, although it was rare that the faintest scribe line could be seen. His finely chiseled letters slant right producing an italic form. Certain lowercase letters – **a**, **d**, **h**, **i**, **k**, **l**, **m**, **n**, **t**, and **u** finish on the base line with a delicate upturned forty-five-degree angled foot. The carver produced tympanum iconography that was simple, often abstract, within the urn and willow motif. These variations on a theme filled my inventory notes during the summers of the late 1970s. Eventually, the survey expanded south and east into the New York counties of Broome and Chenango. Then, there came a time when unexpected images appeared that varied widely from the neoclassical dictates of the day.

In 1979, Laurel Gabel, Research Coordinator of the Association for Gravestone Studies (AGS), visited Cortland and viewed Coffin Man's work. She discussed sources that would be helpful and directed me to continue gathering the carver's inventory, urging me to cross-match the deceased males with probate files. In parting, Laurel encouraged me with the words "*It will only take one stone.*" I felt certain that the "*one stone*" and the coffin carver's name would soon appear.

Shortly afterward, Laurel passed along information about “upright coffins” and “funny faces” reported in Otsego County near Cooperstown, New York. At Milford, New York there were several stones engraved with multiple upright coffins that commemorated infant deaths. Nearby, in Decatur, New York, the hilltop cemetery yielded a treasure among the waist deep weeds. On the double-top marker was displayed a pair of large, disk faces whose disconcerted expressions peered out at me. In truth, the astonishment was mine.

Nabby Lewis & daughter d. 1814/1813
Decatur Cemetery
Otsego Co., NY

Coffin Man had certainly engraved the introductory phrase “Here lies,” and the tight zig-zag design[2] that framed the tympanum and borders. On the other hand, a contemporary artisan seemed to have produced the inscription.[3] I was quite perplexed as to who had carved the disk faces. Each had a double struck, down-turned mouth, and lightly sketched hair. The deeply engraved eyes, cheeks and brow elements led me to visualize a mask. As charmed as I was by these caricature faces, there was nothing, thus far, in Coffin Man’s iconographic catalog of urns and willows that prompted me to attribute these intriguing features to him.

While I was discussing Coffin Man’s work at the 1981 AGS Conference in Schenectady, New York, a voice spoke from the darkness and reported “that carver” had placed stones in Harford, Pennsylvania. The speaker was Ann Hawkins, a stone carver from Washington, D.C. who stopped for a travel break at the Harford Cemetery and admired the carver’s lettering. A rubbing verified her observation. Thanks to Ann’s advice, I’ve discovered Coffin Man gravestones throughout northern Susquehanna County, Pennsylvania including two small profile portraits atop a double marker that memorialized Obadiah Carpenter, 1810, and his wife Ama, 1814.

Obadiah Carpenter d. 1810
Harford Cemetery
Susquehanna Co., PA

John Harmon d. 1812
Afton Eastside Cemetery
Chenango Co., NY

During the tenth year of the search, another AGS member from Norwich, New York, shared with me her large gravestone photo collection. I quickly recognized Coffin Man’s work, particularly a winged, mask-eye, disk face in Sidney, Delaware County, New York, for John Hovey, 1813. The inscription lettering, coupled with the iconography, removed all doubt I had harbored as to whether Coffin Man carved the mask-eye, disk faces. The winged icon and other remarkable and unusual images began to surface persistently. The carver’s territory expanded further east into Otsego County along the Susquehanna River and southeast into Delaware County, New

[2] Carving technique called “walking the chisel.” The rocking-like motion, also directed forward, produces a zig-zag line somewhat resembling the “herringbone” prints left in the snow by a skier walking uphill.
[3] As yet an unidentified carver associate, pseudonym Open Urn Man.

York situated in the foothills of the Catskill Mountains. A mask-eye sun-face resting on the tympanum base line, in Kilroy[4] fashion, appeared on stones in Chenango County, for Harmon 1812, and in Tompkins County, New York, for Bloom, 1818.

Henry Matteson d. 1815
Harford Cemetery
Harford, Susquehanna Co., PA

Mary Dennis d. 1815
Ithaca City Cemetery
Ithaca, Tompkins Co., NY

Carpenter Children d. 1803
Harford Cemetery
Harford, Susquehanna Co., PA

For fifteen years, certain that the next gravestone would enlighten me as to who had inscribed the upright coffins, my eyes scanned each new site for sandstone markers with the half-round crown set on square shoulders that the carver preferred. Ultimately it was serendipity that revealed Coffin Man's origins and the training that influenced his designs. Again, a coffin was involved. During 1986, as I worked toward a degree at the University of North Carolina[5], the research for an honor's thesis yielded an unexpected and startling surprise. A bibliography included a volume of rubbings. I had never expected to see a published picture of a Coffin Man stone. And yet, there in Edmund Gillon's collection,[6] was an exhilarating new lead. My eyes widened as I examined the details. Where was the location of that stone? The answer came from within the inscription – *"Ebenr Dewey ... died ... 1794."*

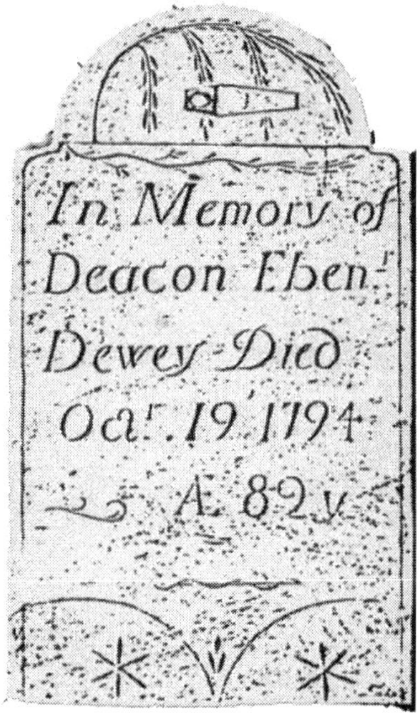

Ebenezer Dewey d. 1794
Dewey Family Cemetery
Royalton, Windsor Co., VT
By Coffin Man

Ebenezer Dewey's death had occurred shortly after the first U.S. Census in 1790.[7] Residing in Windsor County, Vermont, I noted that two residents by that name were living in the Town of Royalton. Soon after my 1987 graduation I traveled to Royalton, eager, after so many years, to discover the carver's name on a gravestone or in the probate records of Windsor County. What I saw in those eastern Vermont burial grounds were the images and designs that had been repeated on gravestones in New York State. Even as Coffin Man's handiwork was all around, his identity continued to be a mystery.

---

[4] "Transit Association Ships a Street Car To Shelter Family of 'Kilroy Was Here,' " *New York Times,* December 24, 1946 - https://www.nytimes.com/1946/12/24/archives/transit-association-ships-a-street-car-to-shelter-family-of-kilroy.html

[5] "Remember Me As You Pass By: The Stone Carvers of Cortland Co., NY," Dexter, M. L. University North Carolina-Chapel Hill, Interdisciplinary Studies Honors Thesis, 1987.

[6] Gillon, Edmund Vincent Jr., Early New England Gravestone Rubbings, New York, Dover Publications, 1966, Plate 121.

[7] Heads of Families at the First Census of the United States taken in the Year 1790, Vol. III, Vermont, Washington: Government Printing Office, 1908.

In the small Dewey graveyard, fallen stones lay embedded in well-manicured grass. I stood over Juda Dewey's engraved stone and a large sun-face stared back at me. There was the mask-eye disk face! Moreover, horizontal coffins that contained nickel-size, mask-eye faces decorated the crowns of many headstones, including that on Ebenezer Dewey's shattered marker. These gravestones confirmed Coffin Man's presence in Vermont. He had executed all the earliest markers at that site. This was my introduction to Vermont's cemetery treasures; however, I quickly came to appreciate that the puzzle, unsolved, had just expanded exponentially.

Juda Dewey d. 1798
Dewey Family Cemetery
Royalton, Windsor Co., VT
By Coffin Man

Coffin Man creations stood in most of the burial sites along the White River Valley in eastern Vermont from the Towns of Hartland and Woodstock, to Sharon, Pomfret, Barnard, the Royaltons, Tunbridge, north to the Brookfields, and on to Williamstown, near Barre. In 1987, as the New England search developed, I initiated a second gravestone inventory during the subsequent summers and revisited New York and Vermont seeking the *"one stone"* that would bestow an identity on the coffin carver. As more time passed, the gravestone territories and the inventories grew.

In Vermont I examined Windsor and Orange County histories along with individual town's history collections. No carver's name surfaced. Annual visits yielded no clues to this elusive carver: no signed grave markers, initials, or probate payments. As the search approached the end of its second decade, I began to lose hope that I would find any historical record to identify him.

The Vermont inventory did disclose that Coffin Man's gravestone production in that locality took place during less than a decade until about 1806,[8] and throughout that time he was associated with another contemporary stone carver. The pair shared both common tympanum images and a large territory in eastern and central Vermont. Which of the pair was the mentor was not fully clear. I observed that the second carver (who I named the "Vermont Carver") produced the more imaginative and inventive images such as bust portraits, mask-eye disk faces, celestial symbols as well as coffins in the horizontal format, many resting on a bier. In New York State the coffin stood vertically below the inscription. The image was imitated, the placement and orientation were juxtaposed.

Judith Durkee d. 1801
E. Brookfield Cemetery
Orange Co., VT
By Vermont Carver

Benjamin Scott d. 1801
Center Town Road Cemetery
Hartland, Windsor Co., VT
By Vermont Carver

[8] Last gravestone carved by Coffin Man in Vermont, Barnard Cemetery, *Sucy Thomas - died July 31, 1805.*

On the other hand, the engraved lettering styles of these two artisans were substantially different. Coffin Man's lettering was consistent, shallow, a delicate italic technique which strongly reflected the epitaph lettering chiseled by local area carvers. The Vermont Carver engraved primarily in a bold block style though he also employed a more graceful letterform where the digits tapered and flowed down to the imagined baseline. Then again, some of his work displayed a combination of the two formats. Both carvers utilized the same quality of schist and slate for raw materials found throughout their territory.

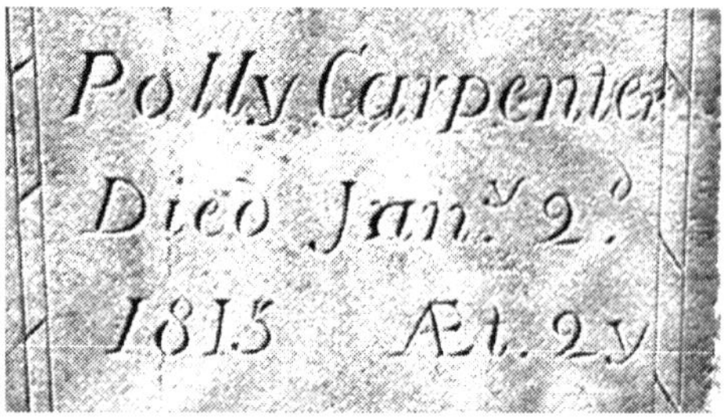

Polly Carpenter d. 1815
Harford Cemetery
Harford, Susquehanna Co., PA
By Coffin Man

Samuel Webster d. 1798
Center of Town Cemetery
Hartford, Windsor Co., VT
By Vermont Carver

In 1988 an Ithaca, New York acquaintance excitedly told me about a marvelous "portrait of a woman" engraved on a nearby gravestone. I was thrilled to encounter the fanciful folk image Coffin Man had chiseled on Mrs. Abegal Doty's 1816 headstone. Her long hair was pulled back, then turned up and held with a clasp. Her long-sleeved dress with tiny buttons and a ruffled bodice were among the charming details engraved on this unique memorial. Historically the male image served both genders in the tympanum. Departing from convention in post 1816, Coffin Man depicted Abegal Doty as a matronly female. The head was reminiscent of his Harford, Pennsylvania busts, as well as the profile portraits created by the Vermont Carver. What induced Coffin Man to replicate a few, seemingly out-of-fashion, quirky icons after leaving Vermont?

Abegal Doty d. 1816
King Cemetery
Ithaca, Tompkins Co., NY
By Coffin Man

My summer searches had produced more than two hundred stones in New York State. An analysis of the expanded inventory disclosed that the carver's operating base most likely lay in southern Chenango County. Coffin Man gravestones appeared in sixty-one New York sites. In the Texas Valley Cemetery, I noted seventeen carved stones and in Coventryville, twelve memorials. An analysis of the inventory, coupled with the discovery of a sandstone quarry close by, and the location of the Bath to Bainbridge Turnpike (a benefit for an itinerant carver) led me to conclude that the carver's operating base lay in southern Chenango County. Determined to discover his identity, I began an investigation into its historical record, looking for clues.

In 1989, while focusing on newspapers of the time period, I discovered an 1824 article printed in the *Oxford Gazette* that reported gravestones being "created and distributed from Miles' Four Corners,"[9] later known as Coventryville.

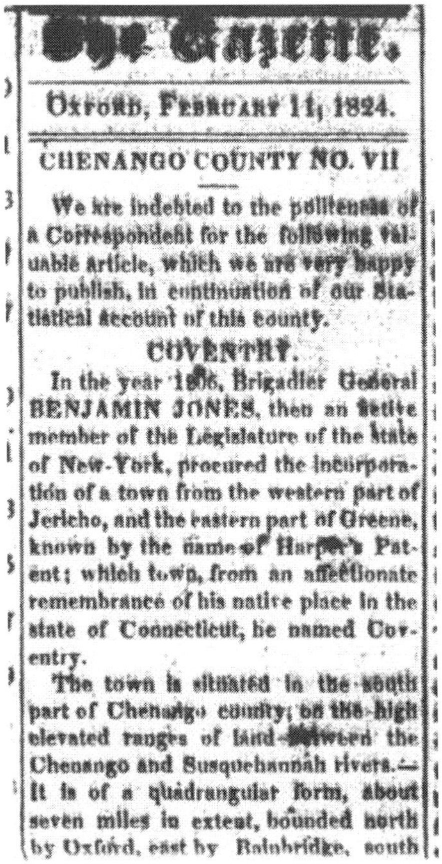

The Gazette.

OXFORD, FEBRUARY 11, 1824.

CHENANGO COUNTY NO. VII

We are indebted to the politeness of a Correspondent for the following valuable article, which we are very happy to publish, in continuation of our Statistical account of this county.

COVENTRY.

In the year 1806, Brigadier General BENJAMIN JONES, then an active member of the Legislature of the State of New-York, procured the incorporation of a town from the western part of Jericho, and the eastern part of Greene, known by the name of Harper's Patent; which town, from an affectionate remembrance of his native place in the state of Connecticut, he named Coventry.

The town is situated in the south part of Chenango county, on the high elevated ranges of land between the Chenango and Susquehannah rivers.— It is of a quadrangular form, about seven miles in extent, bounded north by Oxford, east by Bainbridge, south

The Gazette, Oxford, [NY]
February 11, 1824
Chenango County No. VII

"Coventry . . . Quarries of building stone . . . of dark brown color; . . . and considerable quantities have been wrought into monuments for burial grounds, and disposed of in this state and in Pennsylvania. The stone does not admit a high polish; but can be made tolerably smooth . . ."

The article discussed the Town of Coventry's attributes compared to the recent 1820 Census returns. I guessed that the author might have been Benjamin Jones since his was the only name mentioned specifically. After years of following the gravestone trail, I was elated to finally uncover evidence that made it quite probable that Coffin Man and Coventryville were indeed linked.

To re-examine Coventry's historical documents, I first revisited the Chenango County Historian's record collection at the county seat in Norwich. The search included printed histories, surname files, church records,[10] census schedules, newspapers, tax records, store accounts, school, and miscellaneous records. At the courthouse, I once again scrutinized the property and probate records. I could not find any evidence of who operated the burial monument business at Coventryville. I could feel the fire's heat, but still could not find the flame.

According to the 1820 Census[11] fifteen Heads of Household were engaged in "manufacturing." These Coventry residents were cross-matched with the historical records and the population schedule without success. Had the census taker included gravestone engraving as "manufacturing"? He had not included any detail of raw materials or labor costs for such a business in the extended schedule. Did the carver also operate a farm and fall into that majority category? Again, I contacted Laurel Gabel, of AGS, and read the names to her. She noted that both Stewart and Roberts were known carver families in New England and they should be given a close look. She sensed the answer was close at hand, only "*one stone*" away. The Stewart name produced no paper trail, the Roberts family, promising at the start, soon went cold.

---

[9] The Gazette, 1813-1827, published at Oxford, NY; archived at Burr Library vault, Oxford, NY

[10] Congregational Church History, Town of Coventry Museum at Coventryville, NY

[11] Heads of Families at the Fourth Census of the United States taken in the Year 1820, New York, Chenango County, Town of Coventry, Washington, DC Government Printing Office, 1908.

Through the 1990s, I doggedly pursued that elusive tell-all *"one stone"* and returned to seeking new cemeteries with the square-shouldered sandstone markers. Coffin Man utilized

Betsey Rankin d. 1816
Texas Valley Cemetery
Texas Valley, Cortland Co., NY

Watrous Twins d. 1818
Harpursville Cemetery
Ouaquaga, Broome Co., NY

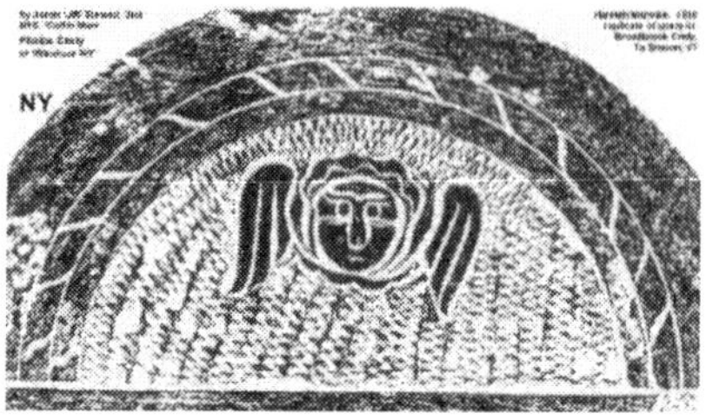

Hannah Manville d. 1810
Lyons Cemetery, Rt 79
N. Windsor, Broome Co., NY

the urn and willow motif predominantly, so when unexpected, whimsical images akin to a face in a moon appeared, they continued to delight and renew my spirit. The folk-art images constituted less than five percent of Coffin Man's work, and I was always excited to happen upon the rare and unusual.

John Hovey d. 1813
Pioneer Cemetery
Sidney, Delaware Co., NY

Sanford Avery d. 1802
Ransom-Kendall Cemetery
S. Woodstock, Windsor Co., VT

These fanciful folk forms, and the repeated use of the vertical coffin icon, are rarely seen outside New England as the eighteenth century closed. I remained curious as to what motivated Coffin Man to carve a precious few of the allegorical facsimiles that harkened back to the Vermont Carver, his companion and possible mentor, during another time and place.

On June 21, 1998, the project's twenty-third anniversary, I made my annual pilgrimage to Coventryville, to the cemetery, the gravestones and the 1820 community I had come to know so intimately. With my research expectations unfulfilled, and my motivation and resolve flagging, I approached the cemetery. I was astonished to see that a major cleanup had occurred and the site sported a fresh haircut. The north end had been cleared of dense overgrowth that, accumulating for decades, had encroached wildly into the yard twelve feet or more. Several long-concealed gravestones had been uncovered, their faces now obscured with dried mud. A wooden stick aided the cleaning and exposing the engraved details. Eagerly I read the inscriptions for five small children's markers.

Standing next to the barbed wire fence, on the cemetery's north boundary, were a pair of large stones. The first I knelt before memorialized Simon Jones, the Town's first white settler who had arrived from Coventry, Connecticut by 1790, and died in Coventry, New York in 1817.[12] A simple urn and willow appeared in an unusual stepped tympanum; however, the stone was unmistakably Coffin Man's work. In place of an upright coffin, under the inscription, he had inscribed a heart.

Simon Jones d. 1817
Coventryville Cemetery
Coventryville, Chenango Co., NY

My thoughts drifted back over twenty plus years to a large heart in the tympanum of a gravestone in Texas Valley. It had drawn my attention to the Coffin Man's work and launched my search for his identity. Remembered also was the name "Benjamin Jones" mentioned in the 1824 *Oxford Gazette* item that had guided me to this place. He was Simon Jones' first cousin. The pair had collaborated as movers and shakers throughout the town's early history. An eerie sensation enveloped me as I prepared my notes for a probate search. There was something special about the Jones' headstone. Often disappointed with such leads, I expected my emotions to be objective and impassive. Instead, I was giddy with excitement as I drove toward the Chenango County Courthouse.

Ascending the stairs double-time at the Courthouse Annex, I located the probate file for Simon Jones' estate and placed it on the archive table. The bound, legal-red envelope was unusually plump and when I released the tie, two cubes of folded paper documents tumbled out. My attention returned to the contents of the envelope. Creditor payments were recorded but the services performed were omitted except for the payment to the maker of the "coffin for $5.00." The room was so quiet I could hear my heart beating. Once more the idiom *"it only takes one stone,"* crossed my consciousness. I paused – *Is this The One?*

I reached for a tightly bound paper packet. The small bundle appeared to be a rare collection of receipts, wrapped with a paper band and secured with a rusted straight pin. There was something spine tingling about the small package. Folded antique, beige receipts slid randomly onto the desktop. It was disquieting to see my hands trembling as the third item was opened and my gaze became riveted to the brown inked words ***"for a pair of G Stones."*** I took a deep breath, read the words aloud, and let my eyes skip to the signature on the receipt– ***"J W Stewart."*** There he was! The Coffin Man was a Stewart. The grave markers with vertical coffins set across central New York State had been executed by J. W. Stewart!

[12] Judd, Oliver P. History of the Town of Coventry, Oxford Review, Oxford, NY 1912, pg. 6.

The moment was simultaneously cartwheel exciting and curiously deflating. My research had been launched from the Texas Valley Cemetery twenty-three years before to fulfill a trivial, nagging curiosity. Coventryville, a focus within my research for more than a decade, had beckoned me to intimately embrace its history and inhabitants and then ironically produced "the stone" which solved the puzzle. The excitement of the moment; however, was short lived. The answer, now in my hand, left me numb. Alone in the probate office, I looked at the receipt signature, and then at the far blank white wall. There were tears as memories flooded in. The cemeteries, the gravestones, summer expeditions, courthouse record rooms, libraries, supportive friends who trekked and searched with me – was it over? Certainly, my life would never be the same because of gravestone carver J. W. Stewart.

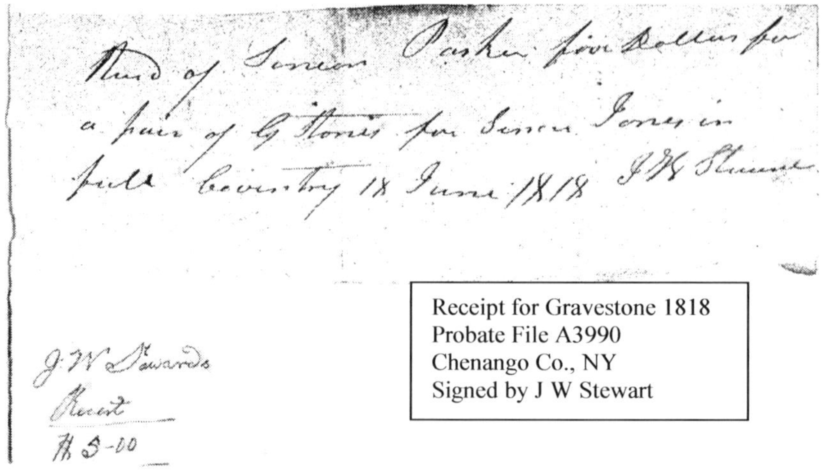
Recd of Seneca Parker five dollars for a pair of G Stones for Seneca Jones in full Coventry 18 June 1818 J W Stewart

J W Stewards Receit $5-00

Receipt for Gravestone 1818
Probate File A3990
Chenango Co., NY
Signed by J W Stewart

The discovery, of course, created a new set of questions. Who was J. W. Stewart, the stone engraver? What did the initials stand for? Did he live in Coventryville, own property, have a family? His work in central New York had ceased with a handful of grave markers dated "1820" and I wondered if he stopped due to death or injury? Did he move further west or return to Vermont and resume his work there?

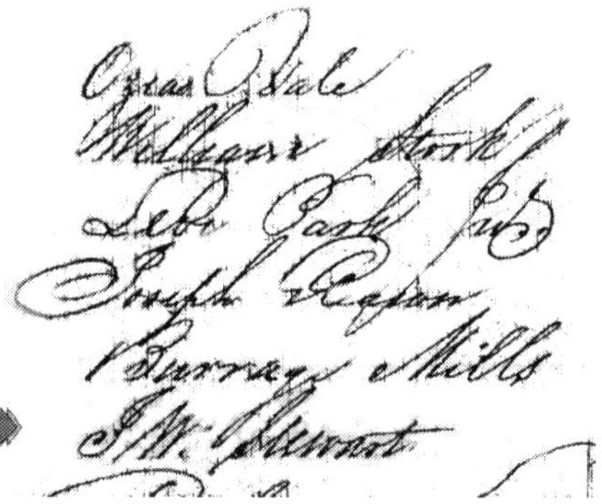

1820 U. S. Census
Tn of Coventry, Chenango Co., NY

Burrage Miles Hotel ca. 1811
Coventryville, New York

J. W. Stewart appears on the sixth line of the 1820 Coventry Census. Contiguous names of pioneer residents confirm that he did reside in Coventryville, in the Miles Corners community, possibly at the Burrage Miles' hotel since the proprietor's name immediately precedes Stewart's in the census. The carver's household included a white female, between 16 and 25 years of age. His age was reported as between 25 and 45, occupation – "manufacturing". If he carved at age eighteen during the mid-1790s in Vermont, he would have been in his mid-forties in 1820, and born between 1775 and 1780.

A deed search revealed that J. W. Stewart had not owned property in Chenango County or any contiguous jurisdiction. I was unable to locate him as a head of household in any succeeding census through 1850 in New York, Pennsylvania, Vermont or New Hampshire. To date, no gravestone carved by J. W. Stewart for any person named "Stewart" has been found in any of the aforementioned states.

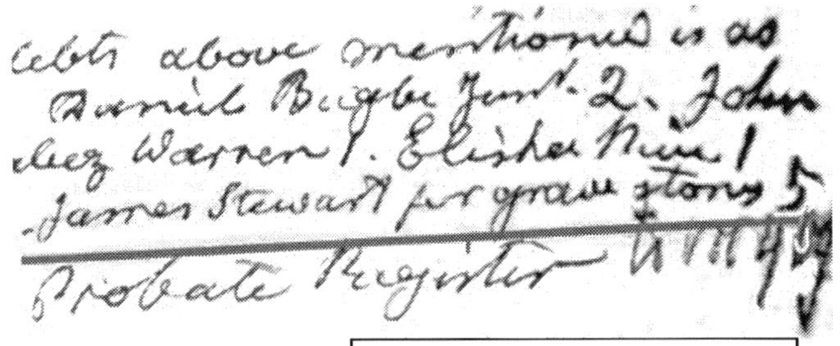

Probate Volume Three, Pg. 246
Woodstock, Windsor Co., VT

With the name "J. W. Stewart" in hand, I returned to Windsor County, Vermont prior to the end of June 1998, expecting to find him there among those records and learn more about his origins. On a rainy day I sought shelter in the Courthouse at Woodstock. While turning the pages of Volume Three of the Probate Record Books,[13] at closing time, I uncovered a five-dollar gravestone payment to a "James Stewart!"

The deceased, Benjamin Bryant of the Town of Hartland, had died in 1801. At the time I considered that "James" was "J. W." At long last, I fully expected the Bryant stone would confirm the work of J. W. Stewart/Coffin Man. Using Vermont Old Cemetery Association (VOCA) maps, I located a burial site on Center Town Road in Hartland, Vermont. As I moved toward the cemetery incline, some late day sunlight caused the meadow apron of wet, green swale grass to shimmer in a gold light. A large, old stone vault held my curiosity as I skirted its partially open iron gate. Not a stately courthouse, nevertheless, the aura of this place, the vault, the light, the solitude seemed magical – what an exquisite setting to end this search.

Benjamin Bryant d. 1801
Center Town Rd. Cemetery
Hartland, Windsor Co., VT

I climbed the arched, grass-covered embankment to find the puzzle's answer. In rapidly fading light my gaze came to rest upon an unanticipated revelation. Benjamin Bryant's large, dark blue slate grave marker had been carved by the Vermont Carver, who now also had a name - James Stewart! I could hardly be disappointed with this unexpected finding. Two Stewart carvers, the familial connection seemed obvious, but the relationship was not yet clear.

[13] Harford Probate District, Windsor Co., Woodstock, VT, Vol. 3, Pg. 246. Benjamin Bryant Estate.

Although James' most familiar images, such as the bottle-cap face and profile portraits were absent from this Bryant headstone, the urn, lettering and other small details confirmed the work of the Vermont Carver. James Stewart is the artisan who shared a territory in eastern Vermont with J. W. Stewart at the turn of the nineteenth century. I looked east across the Connecticut River and reflected on how J. W. Stewart, James Stewart and the Claremont, New Hampshire documented stone carver Jonas Stuart were related. Surely, they were.

Theody Denison d. 1801
Plains Cemetery, Rt 5
Hartland, Windsor Co., VT

Time constraints kept me from crossing the river to sort out these New England Stewarts. With a promise to return later in the summer of 1998, I returned to central New York where the Chenango County Historian's Office personnel proudly informed me that they had found yet another record concerning "their" carver J. W. Stewart. Unpredicted and somewhat unsettling could describe the surprising contents of a nineteenth century audit voucher discovered among some early, uncatalogued court records. The bill, submitted by Constable Loren Sweet, of Coventry, claimed expenses for arresting "on July 31, 1822… Jonas W. Stewart." [14] The record revealed Stewart's given name and partially explained the abrupt end of his carving career in the area. The nature of the charge and the disposition has not been determined.

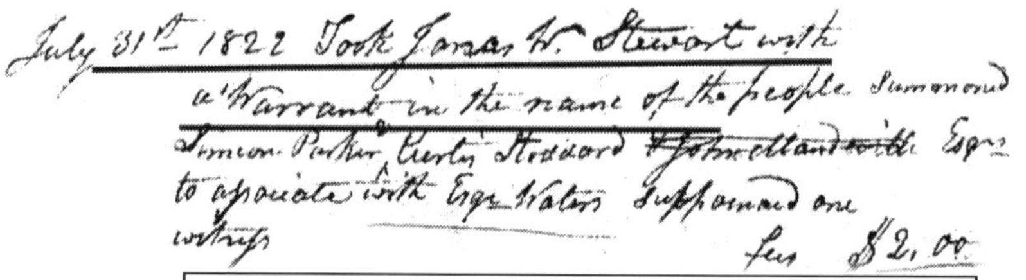
July 31st 1822 Took Jonas W. Stewart with a Warrant in the name of the people Summoned Simeon Parker, Curtis Stoddard ~~[illegible]~~ with Esqr to associate with Esqr Waters Subpoenaed one witness
fees $2.00

Audit Voucher submitted by Loren Sweet

There could be little doubt that Jonas W. and James Stewart must be related to the Claremont, New Hampshire resident stone carver Jonas Stuart who was already known to carver researchers. That winter in Chapel Hill, North Carolina I extracted what had been reported about him. His roots may have been in eastern Massachusetts and he possibly trained in Groton with the William Park family before arriving in Claremont or Charlestown, New Hampshire early in the 1770s. It was alleged he abandoned certain elegant design work for want of clientele with the means to pay suggesting he then carved uninspired, repetitious, tympanum images of plump heads

Kezia Jenison d. 1771
Walpole Village Cemetery, Cheshire Co., NH
by Wm or John Park, not Jonas Stuart [Sr]

[14] Chenango County Historian's Office, 45 Rexford St., Norwich, NY 13815, Miscellaneous Court Records ca. 1820, uncatalogued.

and potted flowers.[15] (Stuart, I am certain, taught himself to carve using the Park images for design information as he acquired his technical skill.)

Atherton Chaffee Sr d. 1776
Old Westminster Cemetery
Westminster, Windham Co., VT
by Jonas Stuart [Sr]

The historical record reported that Stuart traveled to Dorset, Vermont in 1795 and there he carved the newly quarried white marble for a time and possibly trained other carvers.[16] None of the commentaries I located at that time mentioned his extended family.

David H. Chase d. 1794
Trinity Cemetery
Cornish City, Sullivan Co., NH
By Jonas Stuart [Sr]

The following year, in June 1999, I returned to Windsor, Vermont and walked about the old cemetery lying in the shadow of the stately white Old South Church on the main street. The work of Jonas W. Stewart/Coffin Man and James Stewart was not present but countless memorials engraved by the folk carver Jonas Stuart of Claremont dominated the site. It appeared that the Vermont Stewart carvers did not share sites with Jonas Stuart, and vice-versa. Why?

The urgency to explore Jonas Stuart's family tree launched me into New Hampshire without further delay. Almost immediately I happened upon the secluded Trinity Church graveyard, filled with monuments by Jonas Stuart displaying an array of tympanum designs, not just the pumpkin head with its vaulting vegetation, the archetype most often seen in print. Winged faces at this site also seemed to be the work of Stuart, as he was the carver of choice for the distinguished Chase family who were interred there.

At Union Cemetery in West Claremont, New Hampshire, I stood waist deep in Stuart gravestones, the earliest dated 1769.[17] Many tympanums exhibited the familiar, shallowly carved pumpkin head attributed to Jonas Stuart as a result of a probate payment to him by the estate of John Denison[18] for a marker standing in Walpole, New Hampshire. Jonas was an early and longtime resident of Claremont and was enumerated in the 1820 Census. This cemetery was his "home" cemetery and displayed a wide range of death dates from 1769-1820, which spanned his extensive carvings career.

Mary Chase d. 1789
Trinity Cemetery
Cornish City, Sullivan Co., NH
By Jonas Stuart [Sr]

---

[15] Benes, Peter "The Rockingham Carvings: Folk Ecclesiology in the Upper Connecticut River Valley 1786-1812." New England Historical & Genealogical Register, vol. 132, Apr. 1978, pp. 97–114.
[16] Dorset, VT "Marble Quarries (in Dorset)." The Vermont Historical Gazetteer: Magazine, embracing A History of Each Town, Civil, Ecclesiastical, Biographical and Military, 1868, pp. 189-190.
[17] Gravestone of Benadick Roys d. 1769. . . 35 years; bd. Union Cemetery, W. Claremont, NH, "earliest buried."
[18] Keene, NH, Cheshire County Courthouse, Probate File D-20, Estate of Denison, John "paid Jonas Steward for pair of Gravestones 1:8:2."

Also, in Union Cemetery, were more winged heads, a variety of stone types, and other carver's work including that of Gershom Bartlett. The whimsical work of James Stewart also appeared here engraved on a medium grey-blue stone similar in texture to the Bryant probate stone in Hartland, Vermont. Again, I considered relationships – brothers or father and son, an uncle or cousin? I came to realize that thus far I had not seen Jonas W. Stewart/Coffin Man's work at the site. Why not? Later, at the rear of the old section, my eyes glanced toward a solitary grave marker for John Marshal set off under a far tree that displayed an unmistakable design. Jonas W. Stewart engraved that stone! A small second marker was also noted. They continue to be the only examples of his work in New Hampshire that I have located.

Rebedkah Hitchcock d. 1799
Union Cemetery
Claremont, Sullivan Co., NH
by James Stewart

John Marshall d. 1802
Union Cemetery
Claremont, Sullivan Co., NH
By J. W. Stewart, 2nd - Coffin Man

At Claremont's Fiske Library, the historical record concerning Jonas Stuart, stone carver, was scarce. I shared my story with interested staff and they produced a microfilm for the Claremont, New Hampshire Town Proprietor's Record[19] that commenced in 1770. Jonas Stuart's name appeared quite often among the early pages since he filled several minor town positions, i.e. fence viewer. A full day of scanning microfilm was rewarded in the year 1806. The meeting clerk had documented the family of "Jonas Stuart" as part of the Town Record![20] [See Addendum B]

Names and dates from the original document are in **bold lettering**. Bracketed remarks are based on genealogical research for this family.

---- TOWN PROPRIETOR'S RECORD ----

JONAS STUART md. Mary Grimes [married 1766 at Newton, MA; ten children; ca. 1772 – 18??, New Hampshire, Vermont, Massachusetts]

Children:

Samuel was b. 1767; [Newton, MA] [married Lucy Davis, children; possibly d. 1850 Grafton, VT]
Jonas [Jr.] **was b. 1769;** [Newton, MA] [a "Junior" who apparently died before 1778]
Polly, Jr. was b. 1774; [Claremont, NH] [prob married Elisha Spencer, children d. 1843]
JAMES GRIMES was b. Jun 15, 1776; [wife Chloe, children; carved VT, NH ca. 1797-18??]
JONAS [W], 2nd was b. Oct 5, 1778; [carved VT ca. 1796 – 1806; NY, PA 1810 – 1822]
William, was b. 1781;
Sally, was b. 1783;
Alph[onzo] **Converse, was b. 1785;** [Dartmouth grad; to PA; d. 1819 killed in a duel]

---

[19] Ibid., Claremont, NH Town Proprietor's Record, microfilm, 1806, Part ll, pg. 602.
[20] Ibid.,,

Charles Chadwick, was b. 1787; [wife Mary Barnes, children; he d. Wisconsin]
Betsey, was b. 1789;
Note: In this record all the children's last names are recorded as "Stuart."

SUMMARY

Jonas Stewart, 2nd, aka J. W. Stewart, aka Coffin Man. Stone carver, born October 5, 1778, probably at West Claremont, New Hampshire. He was the son of Jonas Stuart [Sr], stone carver, and Mary Grimes, his wife [daughter of James Grimes of Newton, MA], they of the Town of Claremont, Cheshire County [now Sullivan], New Hampshire. His overall carving technique and designs reflect his father's work minimally, i.e. shallow engraving, mask-eye treatment, rope borders and "Here lies." Except for the two stones noted in Union Cemetery, New Hampshire, the balance of his 300+ stone inventory rest in Vermont, New York and Pennsylvania. He is lost from the historic record in 1822.

Rhonda Church d. 1796
Maple Hill Cemetery
Dorset, Bennington Co., VT
by James G. Stewart

James Grimes Stewart. Stone carver, born June 15, 1776, probably at West Claremont, Cheshire County, New Hampshire. He was the son of Jonas Stuart [Sr.], stone carver, and Mary Grimes, his wife, they of the Town of Claremont, Cheshire County [now Sullivan], New Hampshire. His early work compares with his father's designs, then variations occur which led him to his own capricious genre.

James G. accompanied his father to Dorset, Vermont during the late eighteenth century to work with marble being quarried there. (At that site is Ephrim Baldwin's gravestone inscribed "Erected by Asa Baldwin," often misread as "Created by Asa Baldwin." Baldwin was not a carver.) The Claremont 1810 U. S. Census enumerated James Stewart with his young family, as well as an elderly couple believed to be his aging parents. About that time, he and a younger brother, Charles C. Stewart, owned their father's farm in East Claremont, New Hampshire.

William Perry d. 1801
Cushing Cemetery
Woodstock, Windsor Co., VT
by James G. Stewart

James G. set grave markers in western New Hampshire burying grounds alongside his father's work and carved prolifically throughout eastern central Vermont from Chester northeast through Woodstock to Randolph Center and Williamstown from the mid-1790s until about 1813. The inventory is incomplete and continues to grow. This engraver's inventory displays innovative creativity including bust portraits both in high relief and incised, mask-eye bottle-cap faces and celestial renderings in the tympanums. In Chester, Vermont the unique Riggs (1800) three-figure memorial is assigned to him. Where did he go?

Jonas Stuart, [Sr.] was last enumerated in the 1820 Claremont U.S. Census with an elderly female, most probably his wife Mary G. Both are reported between seventy and eighty years of age, living alone. They were married at Newton, Massachusetts in 1766. From about 1772 they resided on Lot 12, in the Town of Claremont and raised a family. About 1792 the parcel was acquired through a transfer that involved their then minor son James Grimes Stewart and a certain James Grimes of Newton, thought to be either Mary's father or brother.

Sometime after 1792, Lot 12 was sold or swapped and the Stuarts settled on a 200-acre farm, parts of Lot 45 and 46, near the town's eastern boundary with Newport, New Hampshire. The property is now very overgrown and needs to be searched for a sizeable stone chip pile to suggest that the shop had also been moved east.

Only two Stewart burials are found in the Broad Street Cemetery at Claremont, behind Fiske Library. James G. Stewart is responsible for engraving these markers for his brother Samuel and his wife Lucy's two sons.

Jonas Stuart, [Sr] carved gravestones for half a century [ca. 1772 – ca. 1823] in Claremont, New Hampshire. Before the turn of the nineteenth century, he carved in marble in Dorset, Vermont. A few gravestones have also been located in eastern Massachusetts near Barre and Hardwick; however, the death dates fall, thus far, within his New Hampshire residency.

From a partial inventory I have categorized Jonas Stuart's gravestone tympanums into three distinct periods :

1] <u>Pumpkin head</u>: 1770 - 1793, two-dimension, incised
2] <u>Cherub face:</u> 1794 - 1801 (with overlap) in modest relief, with ear and chin wings
   Some winged faces with body forms using striations: 1794 - 1805 (with overlap)
3] <u>Urn and Willow</u>: 1803 - 1822, predominantly incised - mix of forms

Throughout his carving career we find a collection of grave markers representing a style not restricted to a particular time period. The quality and creativity of the iconography and lettering, the choice of better stone material, and border column with flame/finial device all reflect great care and superior execution. The subjects are affiliated with religious, social or political standing in town, some deceased are relatives of the aforementioned.

The Willards d. 1797
Forest Hill Cemetery
Charlestown, Sullivan Co., NH

Jonas Stuart, [Sr] died after 1822, probably at Claremont, New Hampshire. His burial site is currently unknown. No record for his probate has been found. I wonder if either of his sons engraved memorial stones for him or his wife's burial location?

Marcy Grout d. 1786
Forest Hill Cemetery
Charlestown, Sullivan Co., NH

Marcy Goodwin d. 1801
Union Cemetery
Claremont, Sullivan Co., NH

Ephraim Noyes d. 1807
Town Cemetery
Enfield, Grafton Co., NH

Hemon Redfield d. 1810
Old Town Cemetery
Claremont, Sullivan Co., NH

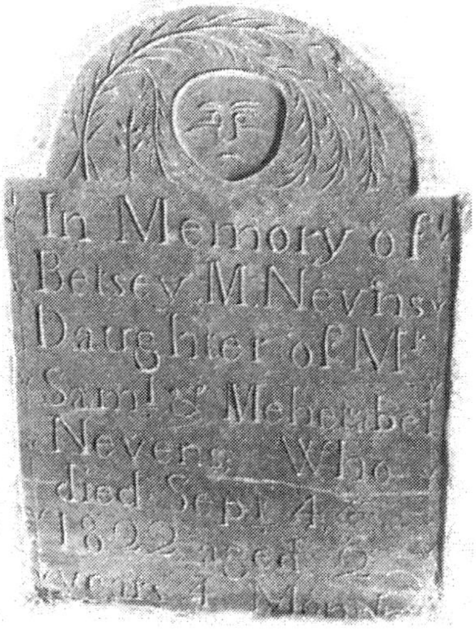

Betsey Nevens d. Sept 1822
Union Cemetery
Claremont, Sullivan Co., NH
Among last gravestones by
Jonas Stuart [Sr.]

Addendum A

<u>THE EYES HAVE IT</u> - A common theme of the Stewart Carvers

By Jonas Stuart, [Sr.] in NH

By James G. Stewart in VT, son of Jonas Stuart [Sr.]

By Jonas W. Stewart, 2nd, aka Coffin Man in NY, son of Jonas Stuart [Sr.]

Addendum B

Town of Claremont Town Proprietor's Record ca. 1806

Proprietor's Recds
Claremont, NH
[microfm @ Fiske Libry]
[Pt II, stmpd pg # 602]

(61) Jonas Stuart

Jonas Stuart and } were married
Mary Grimes }

Births of their children.

Saml Stuart their son was born March 12 1767
Jonas Stuart " " was born Decr 16. 1769
Polly Stuart Jr daughter was born July 5. 1774
James Grimes Stuart born June 15 1776
Jonas Stuart 2nd born Oct 5. 1778 (look in old book
William Stuart born April 18. 1781
Sally Stuart born May 6 1783.
Alph Converse Stuart born March 13 1785
Charles Chadwick Stuart born June 1, 1787
Betsy Stuart Born April 13. 1789.

Addendum C

Freemason Connection

Jonas W. Stewart, 2nd /Coffin Man, carved gravestones across south central New York State, primarily out of Coventryville, Town of Coventry, in Chenango County, New York for about twelve years ending in 1822. I speculate that he was a Freemason who employed the vertical coffin icons and willow on more than half of his markers as a *pictorial signature*, drawing the attention of Freemasons to his body of work. That brotherhood would have recognized the vertical coffin and its companion acacia or willow tree as it related to the organization's large body of symbolism.[21] He may have also been sought out to engrave several "better" stones for deceased Freemasons.[22] In addition, he also included less known freemasonry symbols as tympanum iconography such as: sun and moon faces, seven-star clusters, and crescent moon faces.

Prior to his migration into New York, he carved more than one hundred gravestones in eastern Vermont. As yet, I have located only two memorials with vertical coffins among his work there: three coffins in low relief on a tympanum for a children's stone at Brookfield Center Cemetery and another gravestone with two icons incised on an adult male's stone.[23] At the turn of the century there were conflicted views within the Freemasonry organization. I wonder if that situation influenced his move to New York State and his apparent freedom to use the organization's symbols on more than half of his inventory and bring attention to his work?

4 Grant Children d. 1818
Smithville Flats Cemetery
Smithville Flats, Chenango Co., NY

Henry Bloom d. 1818
Asbury Cemetery
Lansing, Tompkins Co., NY

Jacob Edick d. 1807
Revolutionary War Cemetery
Deposit, Delaware Co., NY

I look forward to continued discussions regarding the Stewart family of gravestone carvers and their body of work. I wish to share my research through this essay. Please give the author the courtesy of citation.

Mary L. Dexter - 2006
mldex9@yahoo.com

[21] Freemasonry, A Journey Through Ritual and Symbol, W. Kirk McNutly. Thames and Hudson, Ltd., London, 1991 Pg. 28-30, 49.

[22] Gravestone for Gen'l Henry Bloom, d. 1818, bd. Asbury Cemetery, Tn. Lansing, Tompkins Co., NY
Gravestone for Solomon Martin, d. 1816, bd. St. Matthews Cemetery, Unadilla, Otsego Co., NY
Gravestone for Daniel Merwin, d. 1820, bd. Bloomville Cemetery, Delaware Co., NY
Gravestone for Ebenezer Wheeler, d. 1813, bd. Partridge Island Cemetery, Tn. Hancock, Delaware Co., NY

[23] Gravestone for Lem'l Parkhurst, d. 1797, bd. Broad Brook Cemetery, Tn. Sharon, Windsor Co., VT

PART THREE

THE STEWARTS: A FAMILY OF GRAVESTONE CARVERS

2020

I've spent the last 45 years actively tracking a family of gravestone carvers across New York, into Pennsylvania, then north to Massachusetts, Vermont, and through New Hampshire. What began as mere inquisitiveness evolved into a web of never-ending connections and far-flung road trips, maps riddled with multi-colored dots, new friends in countless courthouses, and finally a compelling desire to introduce you to these related carvers before I too end up under a headstone. In this essay I will continue the Stuart/Stewart story.

Barto children d. 1819
Texas Valley Cemetery
Marathon, Cortland Co., NY

In the previous section, written in 2006, I told of my search for the identity of the carver I called Coffin Man and how I eventually determined that his name was Jonas W. Stewart 2nd. (Now referred to as JW Stewart to eliminate confusion with his father.) That investigation led me to Vermont and New Hampshire and the discovery that his father Jonas Stuart, Sr. and his brother James Grimes Stewart were also gravestone carvers. I now wish to share with you the additional information that has been uncovered during the past 14 years about this remarkable family of gravestone carvers.

JONAS STUART[24] (1740-1825)

According to Family Memorials . . . Early Settlers of Watertown, Waltham and Weston, MA, John Steward and Hepzibah Hastings were married at Watertown December 11, 1735.[25] Their son Jonas Steward, was baptized at Waltham, Middlesex County, Massachusetts, on November 23, 1740.[26] There is reference to John Steward being a housewright,[27] a trade that built and repaired houses. The couple had two other children, Sarah who married Abijah Richardson at Lincoln, Massachusetts[28] and David Stewart.

---

[24] "Stuart" seems to have preferred this to be the spelling of his surname as noted in the Claremont, New Hampshire Town Proprietor's Record, 1806, page 102. This form is also carved on his son James' gravestone which reads "son of Jonas Stuart" and certain probate payments, Cheshire Co., NH to "Stuart."

[25] Bond, Henry. Family Memorials: Genealogies of the Families and Descendants of the Early Settlers of Watertown, Massachusetts, Including Waltham and Weston; to Which Is Appended the Early History of the Town. Boston: Little, Brown & Co., 1855. Vol. 2, page 792.

[26] Historical Society of Watertown (Mass.). Watertown Records: Comprising East Congregational and Precinct Affairs, 1697 to 1737: Also Record Book of the Pastors, 1686 to 1819. Boston, MA, USA: David Clapp and Son, Printers, 1906.

[27] Tapley, Harriet Silvester. Genealogy of the Tapley Family. Danvers, Mass: Endicott Press, 1900. Page 90.

[28] "North America, Family Histories, 1500-2000" Ancestry.com, Provo, UT, USA: Ancestry.com Operations, Inc., 2016. https://search.ancestrylibrary.com/search/db.aspx?dbid=61157.

As a young man, Jonas served in a local militia belonging to Capt. Jonathan Brown's Company. In 1758 they marched to the area of Lake George, New York during the French and Indian War.[29] The soldiers traveled through the virgin territory of present-day Vermont.

Upon returning home, Jonas Stuart married Mary "Polly" Grimes, on October 27, 1766. She was the daughter of James and Keziah (Chadwick) Grimes of Newton, Massachusetts.[30] Soon after, two Stuart sons were born in Newton, Samuel in 1767[31] and Jonas in 1769. The latter, a "junior" appears to have died young.[32]

Jonas' father-in-law, James Grimes, or his son of the same name, purchased fifty acres, being Lot 12, in the newly created New Hampshire land grant Town of Claremont in 1771.[33] The site required that it be developed within five years and to this end Grimes arranged for his son-in-law to occupy the parcel. Proprietor's records reveal that Jonas Stuart, being one of twenty-one eligible inhabitants, voted in the affirmative in 1771 to call a minister.[34] He is also noted as having registered an earmark for his livestock - "a hole in the left ear." Stuart served variously as the town's field driver, fence viewer, and the collector of the minister's salary including wheat, pork, sheep, and the like.[35] Although not the property owner, he was eligible to vote and surely practiced some useful trade, possibly his father's skill as a housewright, as that would have made him of value to the young Claremont settlement.

Atherton Chaffee d. 1776
Old Westminster Cemetery
Westminster, Windham Co., VT

We do not know what motivated Jonas Stuart to pick up a chisel and mallet to carve his first gravestone. His early life in eastern Massachusetts was lived amid the work of established carvers, including Daniel Hastings and Ebenezer Howard of Newton. Stuart's own style of engraving is not seen there, nor in Harvard or Groton, home of the influential Park family of carvers. His own first efforts can be found in Union Cemetery at West Claremont and in Charlestown, New Hampshire, as well as in Winchester, Rockingham, and Windsor, Vermont.

Elias Olcott d. 1794
Rockingham Meeting House
Rockingham, Windham Co., VT

---

[29] Hurd, Duane Hamilton. History of Middlesex County, Massachusetts: With Biographical Sketches of Its Many of its Pioneers and Prominent Men, Vol. 2. Middlesex: J.W. Lewis & Company, 1890. Page 414.
[30] Ibid.
[31] Newton. Vital Records of Newton, Massachusetts: to the Year 1850. Boston: Pub. by the New England historic genealogical Society, at the charge of the Eddy town-record fund, 1905.
[32] Claremont, New Hampshire. Town Proprietors' Records. Fiske Library microfilm dated 1806, stamped page 602. Handwritten Stuart family document mention of 2nd son named "Jonas" born 1778.
[33] Cheshire, New Hampshire, Deed of Josiah Willard of Winchester, New Hampshire to James Grimes of Newton, Massachusetts, 1771, Book 9 page 159.
[34] Waite, Otis Frederick Reed. History of the town of Claremont, New Hampshire, for a period of one hundred and thirty years from 1764 to 1894, Manchester, N.H.: Printed by the John B. Clarke company, 1895. Page 82.
[35] Cheshire County, New Hampshire. Town Clerk, Town of Claremont Proprietor's Records for May 9, 1771.

These early carving attempts adopted a design used by William Park and his son John of Groton, Massachusetts. Either could have arranged to place the small inventory of their high relief gravestones in the Charlestown, New Hampshire area in the 1770s. Many of these settlers had been Massachusetts residents who had relocated to that outpost known as "Fort Number 4." It appears to have been these images, if not the technical skill, that may have inspired Jonas Stuart to try his own hand at gravestone carving. That occupation, not acquired until his early thirties and apparently self-taught, consumed the rest of his long life. The upper Connecticut River Valley settlements in Vermont and New Hampshire increased rapidly following the War for Independence and Jonas Stuart was well positioned to fulfill that expanding population's inevitable need for grave markers.

Hannah Sartwell d. 1771
Forest Hill Cemetery
Charlestown, Sullivan Co., NH
Carved by Park Family

JONAS STUART'S GRAVEN IMAGES:

Initial Carving Style: (ca. 1772 – ca. 1792/3)

An inventory of Jonas Stuart's earliest work can be found in the Forest Hill Cemetery at Charlestown, New Hampshire, bearing dates between 1772 and 1782. He carved a large roundish face accompanied by two small leaf forms at the cheek, all tucked snugly within a halo-like surround that resembles three-fourths of a space helmet. This "pumpkin-head" image rests on the tympanum baseline and is flanked by vaulting vegetation and flowers emanating from awkward side pots. Low relief borders also attempt to replicate the Park designs by displaying a vertical vine capped with a tulip shape.

Finding worthy stone material appears to have been one of Jonas Stuart's initial difficulties. His early grave markers, carved on undulating, pitted surfaces, left much to be desired. However, by 1780 adequate supplies of acceptable dark gray local schist was uncovered, possibly from a quarry site just north of West Claremont, east of the road to Cornish. Stuart's business, probably on his home property of Lot 12, was near the rushing Sugar River which would have enabled better stone preparation. New slate resources enabled Stuart's shop to fulfill the area's every gravestone requirement. His pumpkin-heads within their halos and framing vegetation can be found in New Hampshire as far south as Swanzey, then north to Hanover, and east as far as Pembroke, near Concord. Before the turn of the century he placed markers in Vermont from Putney north to Randolph Center. Also included are the numerous inland settlements on both sides of the Connecticut River - an amazing breadth of territory of about 60 miles by 70, over four thousand square miles!

Daniel Graves d. 1772
Forest Hill Cemetery
Charlestown, Sullivan Co., NH

Initially, the road systems consisted of primitive tracks and bridle paths which required a sturdy cart, probably drawn by long-horned oxen. To serve the eastern Vermont river towns, Stuart would have had to engage a river ferry or fording to cross the expansive Connecticut River at reduced flow. Although not diverging from his early haloed pumpkin-head design until the early 1790s, examples of Stuart's technical progress with a mallet and chisel is fully on display at Forest Hill Cemetery high on the hill above Charlestown, in Claremont and in Walpole, New Hampshire.

Winged Cherubs: (ca. 1792/3 – ca. 1803)

A brief visit to the Barre and Hardwick area in Massachusetts in the mid-1790s, to place a set of stones for a Jones family in the Buckminster Cemetery, may have been the catalyst for a tympanum design change when Stuart possibly noted that the vacant eyed death's head designs had given way to cherubic faces, many with wings. Could these images have been his motivation to abruptly dismiss the flat, haloed pumpkin-head models? His stones dated 1792 and beyond reveal an updated facial image with modest relief, raised up off the tympanum line, some initially displaying wings at the ear position. Eventually the cherubic face was cradled within the chin positioned wings that joined at the bib. With creative juices flowing, Stuart began to flesh out his souls with abstract body forms using narrow vertical striations beneath these new winged faces.

Olive Hoisington d. 1792
Old South Church Cemetery
Windsor, Windsor Co., VT

Margaret Currier d. 1797
Old South Church Cemetery
Windsor, Windsor Co., VT

Neoclassical Style: (ca. 1803 – ca. 1823)

By the turn of the century, the New England States south of New Hampshire had been experiencing yet another change in preferred cultural taste in images. The Neoclassical period impacted architecture, music, and literature and resulted in gravestone art embracing the urn and willow. Tympanum designs that appear in New Hampshire and Vermont reflect a slow transfer of cultural norms. The Stuart shop finally got around to the urn and willow designs about 1803, but not without a delay in the image interpretation. As the carvers did not have experience with seeing an actual urn, they initially produced odd shaped "folk" images. Within a year or so, change reflected the disappearance of the "balloon image" and gave way to classical urn designs.

William Whiting d. 1800
Broad Street Cemetery
Claremont, Sullivan Co., NH

Daniel Marsten d. 1814
Four Corners Cemetery
Goshen, Sullivan Co., NH

Very Important Person (VIP) Style: Throughout Career

Throughout the span of Jonas Stuart's carving career, there is an inventory of a distinctive style, a group of more ambitious stones. These markers were carved for residents who appear to have risen socially, religiously, or politically within their communities. As a group they are more carefully inscribed, more detailed, and executed on a higher grade of stone materials, which must have added to their cost. A distinctive feature of these grave markers has fashionable side columns, each with a finial flame. This "candle and flame" device appears to be exclusive to these high-market stones.

Moses Chase d. 1799
Chase Cemetery
Cornish, Sullivan Co., NH

Mercy Underhill d. 1794
Maple Hill Cemetery
Dorset, Bennington Co., VT

During the mid-1790s, marble quarries were opened in the area in and around Dorset, Vermont and it is reported that Jonas Stuart was summoned to carve gravestones and possibly train carvers.[36] Found in Dorset, Pawlet and Rupert are many examples of the pumpkin-head as well as winged face designs so often used by Stuart and his son James G. Stewart. Jonas would not revisit the marble medium until 1823, the final year of his carving career in Claremont.

Jonas Stuart's inventory includes many unique images.

Anne Phelps d. 1797
Old South Church
Windsor, Windsor Co., VT

Moses Chase d. 1799
Chase Family Cemetery
Cornish, Sullivan Co., NH

The Cleric Stone * (1793)
Forrest Hill Cemetery
Charlestown, Sullivan Co., NH

***Note**: The Cleric stone's original inscription appears to have been ground off and then recut for "Elizabeth Shepley Willard, 1851." Since the iconography appears to be of a cleric with angels, I hypothesize that the original inscription memorialized Rev. Bulkley Olcott who died in 1793. Rev. Olcott's memorial is now a plain marble tablet standing within the Olcott Family Plot at Forest Hill Cemetery at Charlestown, New Hampshire.

---

36 Middlebury Historical Society (Middlebury, Vt.). The Marble Border of Western New England: Its Geology and Marble Development in the Present Century. Middlebury, Vt.: Published by the Society, 1885.

Stuart's marker for Robert Lane, standing in Newport, New Hampshire, for example, has been penetrated by a large, once shiny nail head possibly to represent the sun's brilliance on this large VIP stone. The actual use of the nail was, in fact, to keep the face of the marker from delaminating, so the nail appears to have served dual purposes.

Robert Lane d. 1794
Pine Street West Cemetery
Newport, Sullivan Co., NH

Displayed on many of Stuart's gravestones is a pear-shape figure that puzzled me for many years. The answer came when I encountered the memorial for Hannah Leverett, who died in 1799. Her grave marker stands in Windsor, Vermont's Old South Church Cemetery. Two containers accompany the winged face, and each exude three distinct forms. I came to understand what the carver's probable meaning for the "pod" form was on so many of his gravestones! We are viewing Stuart's representation for the Cycle of Life: 1. The Bud – birth and new life; 2. The Flower - maturity; and 3. The Seed Pod – death and burial in the grave. Stuart used the pod shape in a wide variety of locations, from the peak of the tympanum to the sides and base of the stones, always positioned with a downward inclination. The Moses Chase stone in the Chase family cemetery in Cornish, New Hampshire is an excellent example of this.

Hannah Leverett d. 1799
Old South Church Cemetery
Windsor, Windsor Co., VT

I uncovered an interesting story about the primitive British outpost Fort Number 4 (later Charlestown, New Hampshire). In August 1754 Capt. James Johnson, his pregnant wife Susanna (Willard) and three children were captured by Abenaki Indians. After crossing the Connecticut River into Vermont, Mrs. Johnson gave birth to a daughter. The captives were marched north through the mountains to Quebec where they remained prisoners of the French for four years. Susanna eventually returned to "Charlestown", married John Hastings Junior and was the mother of seven more children. In 1796 she reported her story in pamphlet form and, after revisiting the Vermont "birth site,"

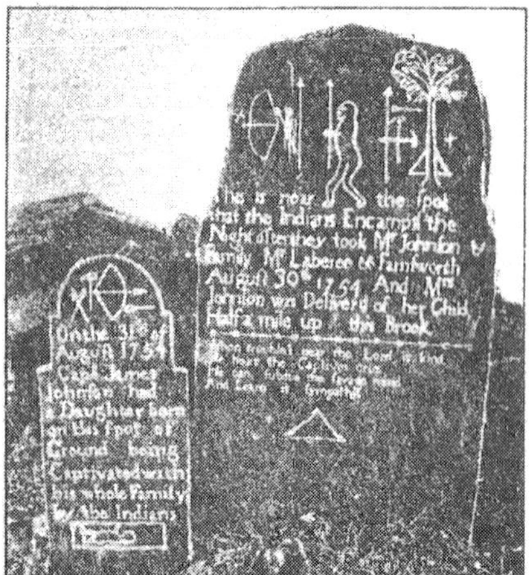

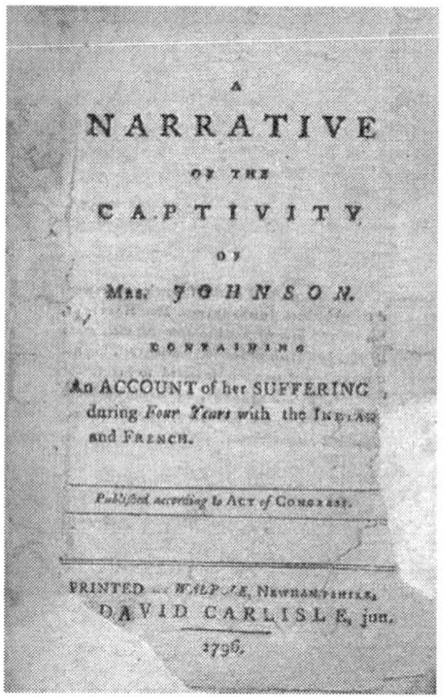
A

NARRATIVE

OF THE

CAPTIVITY

OF

MRS. JOHNSON.

CONTAINING

An ACCOUNT of her SUFFERING, during *Four Years* with the INDIANS and FRENCH.

Published according to ACT *of* CONGRESS.

PRINTED AT WALPOLE, NEWHAMPSHIRE,
DAVID CARLISLE, jun.
1796.

requested that two special stones be engraved telling the tale. The included book image was found in a 1905 edition of Mrs. Johnson's story. Today, the two memorial markers, encased in granite in 1918, recount the captive's narrative. They stand along Route 106 near Felchville, Vermont. It is reported that the "stonecutter" Susanna hired did not place the markers commemorating the 1754 event where she directed. The stone memorials display illustrations of Indian bows, arrows and a quiver, but the story of the Johnson's is in the unmistakable lettering of Jonas Stuart!

Lettering / Numbers / Identifiers

Lettering is the key to identifying Jonas Stuart's widely placed and varied body of work across fifty years. His Garamond style block lettering is narrow and shallowly carved, usually with little, if any, "v-cut" grooving. The one letter that sets ninety-nine percent of Jonas Stuart's stones apart, in the territory where he worked, is the **"Y"** that introduces the ubiquitous phrase "Year of his/her age." The upper portion "**V**" sets fully down on the baseline in a lower-case position. The letter is completed by one single, straight-down chisel stroke below the line.

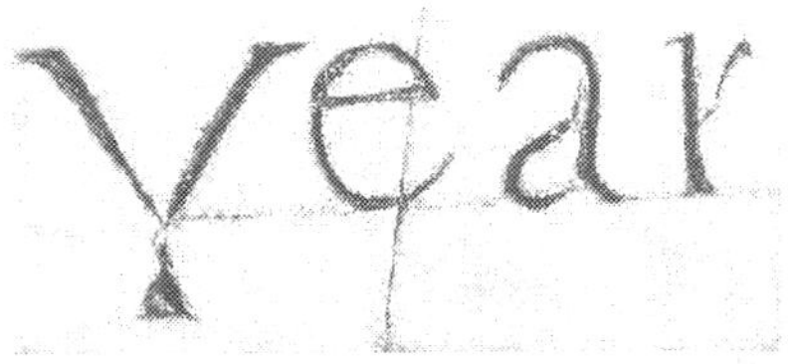

Within the word "Year" the "**e**" uses a straight horizontal line followed by a breast "**a**" form. All other lower case "**y**" within the inscription appear with a left slant tail. More singular forms found within Stuart's inscriptions include a lower case "**g**" with each portion nearly rectangular in form; the bent bar capital "**A**" occurs often; the "**W, w**" are crossed at the center in all instances and a raised, double-loop, "rolled **d**" usually follows the numbers two and three, denoting 2nd or 3rd. Among Stuart's numbers are an open sail "**2**", a Roman nose "**4**" and the distinctive, original unicycle "**5**", tilted forward, with a dipped cap.

His Garamond-like block lettering, an unerring identifier, remained reassuringly static for fifty years.

A high percentage of Jonas Stuart's stones display an epitaph, sometimes a stock format and at other times a combination of lines from familiar verses. Occasionally the information is poignant and speaks of the subject's life or death circumstances.

Stuart's early preferred introduction was "Here lies", with an occasional "Erected to the Memory of" or the attention getting "Hark." "In Memory of" became the preferred incipit by 1800.

Jonas Stuart produced very few gravestones beyond 1820. I uncovered a probate for a pair of marble stones ordered for Daniel Ford, who died in October 1822. This may have been his last carved stone.[37] In the spring the executor rented a horse, traveled to the shop near Newport and took possession of the stones. The surrogate was on his way to set the stones himself in Union Cemetery at West Claremont. He paid Samuel Stewart, Jonas' eldest son who may have been an agent for his father since I find no inventory to suggest that he was a carver; however, he always seemed to reside close to his father. This may have been a final gravestone transaction at the Stuart Shop. Samuel and Lucy (Davis) Stewart and their family eventually moved to Windham, Grafton County, Vermont where he died in February of 1850.

<u>Probate Payments for Gravestones to Jonas Stuart/Steward Cheshire County, NH</u>

- Crafts, John File C-76 Walpole, NH 1791 "May 10 Cash paid Jonas Stuart for making Gravestones. £1:9:2"

paid Jonas Stuart for making Gravestones

- Dunlap, Robert File D-53 1801 Chase Cemetery, Cornish NH "pd Jonas Steward [sic] as per receipt $9.00"
- Dennison, John File D-20 Walpole, NH 1788 "Paid Jonas Stuart for a pair of Gravestones" £1:8:2
- Farwell, Isaac File F-33 Charlestown NH "1792 Jan 28 Jonas Steward [sic] £3:0:0"
- Ford, Daniel File F-182 Claremont NH 1822 "Jonas Stuart for a pair of gravestones."
- Emerson, Hezekiah File E-19 Four Corners Cemetery, Goshen NH 1806 . . . "for a pair of gravestones . . ." Tympanum [masonic items] & lettering by Jonas Stuart . . .

[37] New Hampshire, County Probate Estate Files, 1769-1936, <u>FamilySearch</u> (https://familysearch.org/ark:/61903/3:1:3QS7-L9WH-KD9L?cc=2040042&wc=M7M1-7M3%3A383109201%2C383928001 : 22 May 2014), Cheshire, Case no F143-F205 1816-1826.

The 1820 Claremont U.S. Census had enumerated Jonas Stuart and his wife, ages in the "80 to 90" category, for a final time at Claremont, still reporting his occupation as a "manufacturer." The Stuart Shop apparently closed in 1823 and Jonas and his wife moved on to Cabot, Vermont following the earlier path of son James G. The same question arises with regard to who was at that location that beckoned them to make that journey. Possibly there was a family member, a married daughter or granddaughter. There are no "Stuart" or "Stewart" property records found.

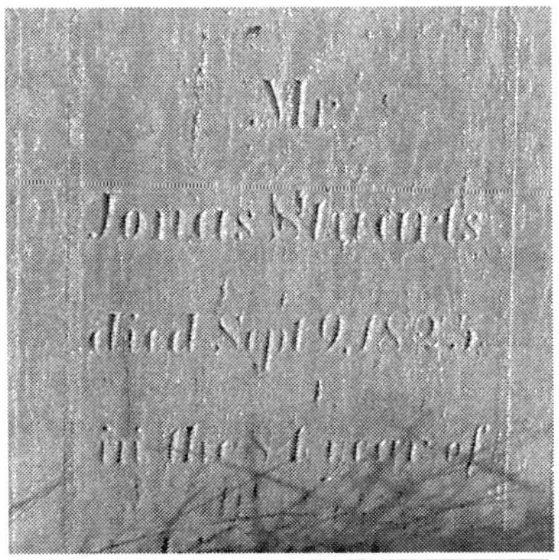

Jonas Stuarts d. 1825
Center Cemetery
Cabot, Washington, Co., VT

A small posting published in the November 3, 1825 edition of The North Star reported that Mr. Jonas Stewart had died after a short illness, in the 85th year of his age.[38] At Center Cemetery, east of Cabot, a gray-green marble gravestone reads "Mr. Jonas Stuarts [*sic*] died Sept 9, 1825 in the 84th year of his Age."

The fifty-year Stuart/Stewart family carving cycle ceased. Jonas Stuart's son James was deceased and younger son JW Stewart was no longer in business in Coventryville, New York after his 1822 run-in with the law. His whereabouts remains a mystery.

JAMES GRIMES STEWART (1776 – 1814)

Rebekah Hyde d. 1798
Randolph Center Cemetery
Randolph Center, Orange Co., VT

The third son of Jonas Stuart and the brother of Coffin Man/Jonas W. Stewart, 2nd, James Grimes Stewart has been identified as a gravestone carver through two probate records. One five-dollar payment was issued for Benjamin Bryant's gravestone that stands in the Center Town Road Cemetery in the Town of Hartland, Windsor County, Vermont.[39] A second payment is noted as received from the John Paine estate and appears in James Stewart's own probate record on file at St. Johnsbury, Washington (formerly Caledonia) County, Vermont.[40]

Israel Richardson d. 1799
Cushing Cemetery
Woodstock, Windsor Co., VT

---

38 *North Star*. Danville, Vermont: Ebanezer Eaton, 1807. Vol XIX, Number 45, Page 3.
39 The Estate of Benjamin Bryant. Harford Probate District, Windsor County, Woodstock, Vermont, Vol. 3, Page 246.
40 The Estate of James G. Stewart. Washington County [formerly Caledonia Co.,] Probate District, Washington Co., Vermont, Vol. 7, pp. 406 – 411.

The majority of his carving inventory is in Vermont from Chester in the south, north to Westfield, near the Canadian border. His early work commenced about 1794 and is found near Springfield, then north and west in the region of the White River Valley. Many of his striking, high relief, profile portrait images are seen at Randolph Center. The total inventory of these bust profiles, both incised and in relief, number about fifty.

Stephen Riggs d. 1800
Brookside Cemetery
Chester, Windsor Co., VT

The Tears of America – Bandana
Image by Heritage Auctions, HA.com

At the turn of the century he translated an image from a textile[41] rendered in commemoration of President Washington's 1799 death onto a tympanum design. This unique image was for Stephen Riggs, a young Navy veteran, who was laid to rest in 1800 in Chester, Vermont's Brookside Cemetery. A similar rendering of this scene is accompanied by a verse that gives voice to the triumvirate surrounding Washington's urn: "*Columbia [right], lamenting the loss of her son,/Who redeem'd her from Slavery & Liberty won,/While Fame [trumpeting angel], is directed, by Justice [left] to spread,/The sad tidings afar, that Washington's dead.*"[42] We are left to speculate as to who had access to the print image - the family or the carver?

At that time the Stuart Shop was engaged with engraving the new neoclassical urn and willow design. To assist local residents in identifying these models, James Stewart produced three markers with different renditions of the urn form and in each tympanum, he included the words "an urn" for those not familiar with it.

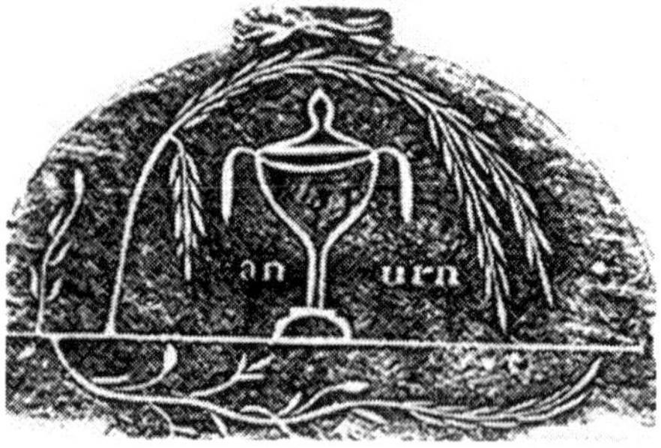

Elizabeth Kibbe d. 1805
E. Randolph Cemetery
E. Randolph, Orange Co., VT

Stewart's work also appears alongside his father's in New Hampshire until 1810. Some of those sites include Union Cemetery and Broad Street Cemetery in Claremont; Pine Street and North Newport Cemetery in Newport; East Unity Cemetery, East Lempster Cemetery and Four Corners Cemetery in Goshen. Only two gravestones carved by brother JW Stewart appear standing with his father and brother's work in Union Cemetery. All three may be found in East Unity Cemetery as well.

[41] Seen by author on a bandana shown on PBS Antiques Roadshow (episode 1310) at Chattanooga, Tennessee July 19, 2008.
[42] Baker, William Sophn. The Engraved Portraits of Washington: With Notices of the Originals and Brief Biographical Sketches of the Painters. Lindsay & Baker, 1880. Page 192.

In late 1809, James Grimes Stewart and younger brother Charles Chadwick Stewart purchased their father's farm, then in the eastern portion of the Town of Claremont, near the Newport town line. James Stewart is noted as the Head of Household in the 1810 Claremont U.S. Census which included an elderly couple, no doubt his parents.[43] The partnership did not last long as Charles purchased James' share in the property in late 1810 and the latter moved to Cabot, Vermont. It is unclear why he and his family made that transition.[44]

Joseph Edwards d. 1807
Center Cemetery
Cabot, Washington Co., VT

James Grimes Stewart produced at least seventy gravestones while residing in Cabot but he no longer rendered the quantity of creative and inventive tympanums, most exhibit simple fan forms. His lettering remained recognizable throughout his carving career.

Lettering / Numbers / Identifiers

Some of his identifiers include a "**German helmet urn**", in addition to his many profile **busts**. The carver seemed to have difficulty with his capital "**M**" meeting the top of the right leg. To preface the deceased's age, the carver often uses "**aet**" in ligature form. The lower loop of the small "**g**" expresses a "**thorn**" on the right side. The small "**y**" has a very stubby tail. The "**5**" is standard using a "**comma**" shaped hat. His brother, JW, preferred the backward comma. James used a rocking-back ampersand.

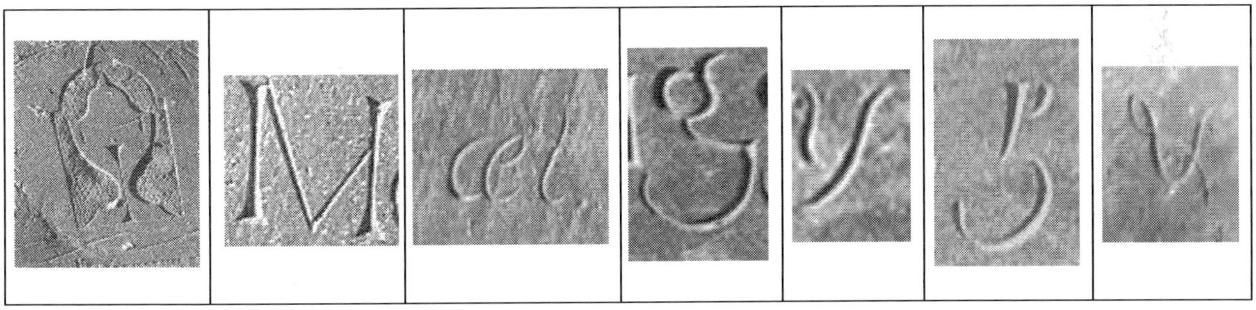

On November 23, 1814 he died at the age of 39. His father engraved a very large, tablet-form gravestone which stands in Center Cemetery, Cabot, Washington County, Vermont and it reflects Jonas Sr.'s continued preference for the surname spelling "James . . . Son of Jonas and Mary Stuart."

---

[43] United States Census Office. Population Schedules of the Third Census of the United States, *1810: New York.* Washington: National Archives, National Archives and Records Service, General Services Administration, n.d.

[44] Cheshire, New Hampshire, Deed of James G. Stewart of Claremont, New Hampshire to Charles C. Stewart of Claremont, New Hampshire, 1810, Book 61, Page 3.

There is a twelve-page probate file[45] for James G. Stewart's estate accounting for the usual expected paperwork; however, the small monetary value required at least three inventories. Within this extensive file we note that James was treated for "an illness" by Dr. Hains which suggests to me that his death at an early age was probably not the result of an accident. His inventories included: gravestones, a saddlebag with tools - which were sold, a horse and a small amount of household items that his widow petitioned to receive. No guardianship papers were submitted. Two outstanding, uncollectable debts, include $7.00 owed by his young brother Alphonzo who was at Dartmouth College at the time and a $40 debt owed by a "David Stewart of Kelly Vale." This last item might have involved a son by that name or possibly an uncle, the younger brother of his father Jonas.

Susan Heath d. 1804
Center Cemetery
Cabot, Washington Co., VT

JONAS W. STEWART, 2nd (1778 - unknown) aka COFFIN MAN

Jonas W. Stewart, 2nd was the fourth son of Jonas and Mary (Grimes) Stuart and the younger brother of James G. Stewart. Initially he placed many stones in burying grounds along Vermont's White River Valley beginning about 1796 with no inventory seen for apprentice work. About 1810, he and his brother James left the oversight of their father's shop at Claremont, New Hampshire, at approximate ages of 32 and 34 respectively. Both continued to carve gravestones. The inventory for JW Stewart appeared in south central New York State and Northern Pennsylvania about 1810, although he is not recorded in the census for that year. He is the "Coffin Man" carver whose name I searched for more than twenty years. As his inventory continues to expand, it is clear that he was an eclectic and talented engraver of death memorials from the turn of the nineteenth century until 1822.

As recently as 2017 I had no reason to believe that this carver left his operating base in Coventryville, New York and returned to New England. Computers and the internet have made it possible to expand searches for any carver's inventory. With these tools, we recently discovered a second New Hampshire cache that indicates that JW Stewart did, in fact, return to New Hampshire to carve and placed at least thirty grave markers in and around Warner, in Merrimack County between 1816 and early 1818.

There exists a signed receipt for a gravestone dated the 18th of June 1818 for the Simon Jones probate item which places Stewart in Coventryville, New York on that day. Since no stone by JW Stewart has been

[45] The Estate of James G. Stewart. Washington County [formerly Caledonia Co.,] Probate District, Washington Co., Vermont, Vol. 7, Pages 406 – 412.

found after that date in the Warner area, we can assume that his thirty stone New Hampshire group was ordered and carved prior to that 1818 date.

It should be pointed out that Stewart also has a sizeable, strong inventory of stones for the 1816 through 1819 period in south central New York State and this presents a conflict which is difficult to explain. If there was one gravestone in New Hampshire by JW Stewart dated after June 1818 I would consider the possibility that his arrest in 1822 might have been about not supplying the Simon Jones' marker as ordered in June 1818; however, the facts do not support that supposition.

What drew JW Stewart back into New Hampshire? Why did he return to that particular area thirty miles east of Claremont, while his father Jonas Stuart was also still carving and placing stones in the same area, as far east as Pembroke, near Concord?

Lettering / Numbers / Identifiers

JW Stewart consistently produced lightly etched, right slant italic-like lettering on his New England work. I found no apprentice letter forms in Vermont where his first engraved stones appear in the White River Valley towns during the decade which possibly began in the mid-1790s. His inscriptions in New York State and Pennsylvania, through 1821/2, reflect his initial work within his father's jurisdiction.

Some of the important letter and number forms that appear throughout Stewart's nearly thirty-year career include the forty-five-degree foot that appears on all small letters that rest on-the-line such as "**a**, **d**, **h**, **i**, **k**, **l**, **m**, **n**, **t**, and **u**." The oval **"e"** form is consistent and the **"AE"** ligature precedes most ages. The **"5"** uses a backward comma in the hat position (brother James used the standard comma.) Final **"d"** is usually rolled left. **"Here lies"** introduces at least half of Stewart's inventory. Most urns are abstract forms and the ampersand is shaped like a "U". Of course, his little vertical coffins at the bottom of his stones are his most notable identifiers.

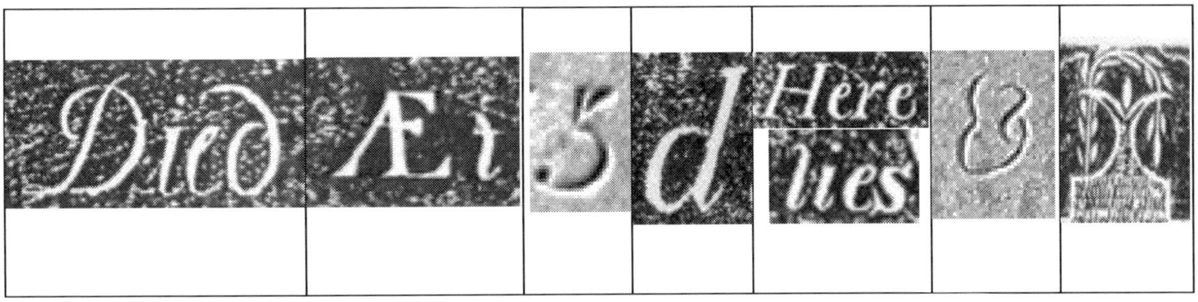

My niece, and now research assistant, Kathleen O'Connell of Cortland, New York discovered an exceptional gravestone for Nancy Osgood and her child by using the Find-A-Grave website. They died in late March 1817 and are buried in Warner, New Hampshire's Old Village Cemetery. The Osgood rendering is striking and displays the carver's outstanding ability with a chisel on stone. The image displays a well-dressed female figure standing to the right of a gravestone, with the bottom third of the blank grave marker visible. A comparison of the carved stone shown on the memorial and the actual gravestone are uncannily similar, including the horizontal line on the carved image that mirrors its placement in the ground. Stewart rendered a female clothed in a waist jacket with button detail, ruffled bodice, full length pleated skirt and shoes. The woman is posed with her right hand near the stone's tympanum, her left hand at her side is clutching a handkerchief. The detail in the work strongly suggests a "personal" knowledge and possible relationship between the carver and the deceased, although I have been unable to substantiate that theory. Who does the woman represent? The deceased? Her mother or sister? I suppose one should not read too much into this likeness, especially when we look into the engraver's array of images.

Nancy Osgood d. 1817
Old Warner Cemetery
Warner, Merrimack Co., NH

Within the carver's existing inventory are two particular gravestones exhibiting nearly identical head profiles. My initial observation, many years ago, was of the head on Cloe Austin's 1800 memorial at Tunbridge, Vermont and then a second image at Ithaca, New York for Abegal Doty who died in 1816. Each of the three cameos display a profile countenance facing left with a very pointed chin, a single mask-eye detail and hair turned up and caught in a clasp.

Cloe Austin d. 1800
Hutchinson Cemetery
Tunbridge, Orange Co., VT

Abegal Doty d. 1816
King Cemetery
Ithaca, Tompkins Co., NY

As previously noted, following his arrest in July 1822 in the Town of Coventry, JW Stewart disappears from the historical record. We do not know the charge levied against him, nor the sentence, but it is apparent that JW Stewart left Chenango County, New York in the summer of 1822. What became of him is still not known and invites more research. Did he continue to engrave stones? Will we ever cross his path again?

The mystery of the J. Stewart signature

Betsey Hurd d. 1818
Pine Street Cemetery
Newport, Sullivan Co, NH

The gravestone for Betsey Hurd, who died in 1818 and is buried in the Pine Street West Cemetery near Newport, New Hampshire, is engraved with well executed *cursive* lettering. The tympanum displays a well-formed urn and willow and at the lower right base of the stone, in Garamond lettering, is engraved "by X J Stewart." In addition to this stone, I have photographed at least ten other markers that are also fully inscribed in the same cursive font. Other miscellaneous stones exhibit single cursive words.

Carver researchers have accepted this "signature" to mean that Jonas "Stewart" of Claremont, New Hampshire engraved this stone and others like it in that vicinity of Cheshire, now Sullivan County, New Hampshire. I would like to suggest that Jonas Stuart [Sr.] **did not** engrave the inscription on these cursive lettered stones and propose an alternative engraver's name.

Jonas Stuart was the father of two sons who were both accomplished stone engravers. Since James G. died in 1814, he is eliminated from this discussion.

Jonas W. Stewart, 2nd, aka "Coffin Man" left New England and established a business in Coventryville, Chenango Co., New York around 1810. Until recently I had dismissed him as well due to his noted location in south central New York State. I have recently learned that he did, in fact, return to eastern New Hampshire about 1816-1818 and, theoretically, could have carved the cursive lettered stones. However, I have not seen any indication that he used the cursive font on any of his more than four hundred stone inventory.

Clarissa Swett d. 1818
Broad St. Cemetery
Claremont, Sullivan Co., NH
By Sears Bryant

Jonas Stuart is on record as showing a preference for the spelling of his surname "Stuart" as noted previously in this essay. Why would he revert to the "Stewart" spelling in this instance? Jonas Stuart was nearly eighty years old in 1818-1819 when these cursive lettered stones appear and I cannot believe that he would have been able to, or desire to, alter his lettering style so radically at that point in his long carving career.

So, why is the Hurd stone "signed?" I believe this signature refers to the "J. Stewart" business! That brings up the question – who was working in the shop that would have engraved these unusual stones? I believe the engraver may have been a man named Sears Bryant. Born in 1771, he was the son of Sylvanus Bryant of nearby Cornish, New Hampshire. He engraved and signed the large gravestone for Dolly True who died in 1817. That stone, and others like it, stand in Mill Cemetery, Meriden, Town of Cornish, New Hampshire and provide unique samples to identify his work.

The inventory for Jonas Stuart, after his sons departed in 1810, continues in the hundreds while his territory changes to more northerly and easterly site placements. Across his territory we see Stuart's lettering continuing unchanged; however, the tympanums take on a new vision which I have described below. These changes appear to be the work of Sears Bryant – a lot of this work!! Once the observer becomes aware of the variety of design combinations, we can readily assign the tympanums to Bryant. From around 1810, for Jonas Stuart's final decade of carving, the following unique tympanum designs of Sears Bryant's on Stuart's lettered stones show a collaboration of the two carvers:

- Deep, tight "walking the chisel," especially outside the central image, i.e. heart, and urn
- Urn is well formed often with side drape, and good interior design
- A central vertical line through the image of the urn or heart
- Multiple use of six-point stars with a single slit-line in each extension
- Neck of urn at times extended
- Use of thin, wavy line for accent, sometimes within the urn
- Urn stands under an arch or point-top-box, thin wavy line fills exterior from urn to edge
- Use of wave and dash decoration, at urn base or in circle around six-point star

There are also several stones completed by Bryant from his own inventory in which the first line below the tympanum reads "In Memory of" in the same *cursive* format as the Hurd stone. (See Ephraim Gay d. 1817 at Old Main St. Cemetery, New London Co., NH)

In 1823 Stuart closed the shop. He moved to Cabot with his wife and died there in 1825. It is noted that Sears Bryant also died in 1825 and is buried in the Huggins Cemetery, Town of Cornish, New Hampshire with others of his family who lived close by on Bryant Brook Road.

PART FOUR

OPEN URN MAN CARVER: APPRENTICE TO COFFIN MAN

2020

I first became aware of the carver I named "Open Urn Man" in the Cincinnatus Village Cemetery, Cortland County, New York, while viewing stones by JW Stewart. The large urn in the tympanum was undecorated. Days later this same carver was again seen at Texas Valley in the Town of Marathon and there was little urn decoration, thus my pseudonym stuck. However, as my research territory expanded to the south and east in New York State, more markers turned up, many with the large urns, but these were at times filled with decorations. I couldn't think of a more appropriate name at the time and elected to stay with the moniker.

Edward Gee d. 1822
Cincinnatus Cemetery
Cincinnatus, Cortland Co., NY

Each summer's research produced more inventory continuing in an ever-widening arc of discovery. At an AGS conference in Schenectady, New York in 1981 I introduced my topic involving "Coffin Man" and was informed by Ann Hawkins that the carver's work was "seen at Harford, Pennsylvania while en route to the meeting." That information sent me further south across the state line where I again observed a sizeable quantity of gravestones for both JW Stewart and Open Urn Man in the New Milford and Harford cemeteries.

Mary McDowell d. 1800
Riverside Cemetery
Chemung, Chemung Co., NY
By Open Urn,
(looks-like Stewart)

Both carvers displayed mature work but were quite different in their style of stone monuments. JW Stewart's work exhibited sharp engraving; however, it was quite shallow as opposed to Open Urn Man's etching that was deep, bold, and expressed few coffins. Most of his inventory revealed vines, flowers, and distinct side columns, whereas JW Stewart placed relatively plain, small abstract urn forms in the tympanum and continued putting vertical coffins at his stone's base. Except for sharing quite a few of the same graveyards, I failed to consider that their relationship might be a craftsman and his apprentice working out of the same shop. Open Urn's stones, on the whole, were larger (approximately 40 to 48 inches tall by 20 inches wide) and most utilized a different, better quality sandstone, many were finished off glassy-smooth.

In New York State, these carvers were discovered to have territory that expanded still further east, and I eventually visited the cemetery at Coventryville in the Town of Coventry in southern Chenango County. The site was an epiphany! There were many Open Urn gravestones but some were much smaller than I was used to seeing and these added to my confusion with regard to who had engraved what.

Lydia Lacey d. 1809
Lacey Cemetery
Laceyville, Susquehanna Co., PA

There was an A-HA moment! Open Urn Man seemed to have begun his carving career at Coventryville in JW Stewart's shop. There was a collection of work by the Open Urn Man carver, relatively smaller stones that produced a "looks-like Stewart" effect in both lettering and design work. As Open Urn learned to carve, it appears he mimicked JW Stewart's style. In some cases, it is apparent that both carvers may have worked on the same stone and displayed their individual styles; one carved the tympanum and iconography, the other carved the letters. This can be very perplexing to the observer.

Continued years of research in an ever-expanding territory determined that there are at least 250 stones by the Open Urn Man. As the portfolio expanded, I searched county probate records without success for adult males with markers by these two carvers.[46]

Roxy Bulkley d. 1810 (marble)
Coventryville Cemetery
Coventryville, Chenango Co., NY

In an article found in the *Oxford [NY] Gazette* from February 11, 1824, the author had commented directly on the fact that there were "burial monuments being made at Miles' Four Corners [aka Coventryville] and they were being distributed both in New York and Pennsylvania."[47] I extended the research trips even further south and then west across Susquehanna, Wyoming, Wayne, and Bradford Counties in Pennsylvania. This produced many exciting markers within his expanding inventory. A few were the smaller looks-like Stewart stones but the majority were large, beautiful engravings on pink/gray, glass smooth products with urns that were filled with decorations! One of these monuments, in the Laceyville, Pennsylvania cemetery, displays an urn that fills the stone from tympanum to base, stunningly decorated in its entirety.

The Open Urn carver appears to have resided in Coventryville which is central throughout his career. We first notice his work about 1815 where his apprentice inventory shows up as looks-like Stewart stones. He remained after Stewart left in 1822 and produced gravestones into the 1830s, including many marble tablets. He supplied a striking sandstone marker for Benaiah Loomis, who died in 1838, the latest date found for his work. This stone, in the Ten Broeck Cemetery near Brisben, New York, has been disfigured by the mounting of a DAR brass plaque which covers the tympanum.

---

[46] Probate searches should include widows as well.

[47] Morgan, Chauncey. Oxford Gazette (Oxford, N.Y.: 1813). Oxford, N.Y. Archived at Burr Library vault, Oxford, NY

At Coventryville Cemetery there is a breathtaking similarity to the large stones for Amasa Ives and Benjamin Benedict, who both died in 1823. When looking at the urns, curved arches and "In Memory of" lettering on these two gravestones, one can only guess that Open Urn and Eclectic Man worked in tandem. The deceased were involved in the establishment and construction of the local church in the late eighteenth century.

Amasa Ives d. 1823
Coventryville Cemetery
Coventryville, Chenango Co., NY
By Open Urn

Benjamin Benedict d. 1823
Coventryville Cemetery
Coventryville, Chenango Co., NY
By Eclectic Man

Open Urn's style changed after Stewart disappeared from the area in 1822. This carver began to engrave deeper for both lettering and decoration and found his own unique voice when cutting his urn, willow and tomb designs. Stewart's leaving allowed the two apparent associates, Open Urn Man and Eclectic Man to divide his general territory. Open Urn continued his work in Chenango, Delaware, and Broome Counties of New York's Southern Tier. In northern Pennsylvania he found a lucrative business in the settlements that included Sheshequin, Wysox, Towanda, Wyalusing, Lynn, and Tunkhannock, and many others that bordered the Susquehanna River. He also seemed to have followed Stewart's journey to Bethany and Pleasant Mount in Wayne County, Pennsylvania. Eclectic Man primarily moved west into Tompkins and Cayuga Counties in New York. The Coventryville shop did not disburse work to the north since the Crandall family, the Hubbard brothers, and other artisans were filling that niche.

I had hoped that the 1830 federal enumeration for Chenango County's Town of Coventry would show each resident's occupation, as in the 1820 and 1840 census. Its omission is disappointing as it would have been helpful in offering us a potential list of "Manufacturers" and offer a clue to Open Urn's identity. I have not found an 1835 New York State census. Isolating individuals residing at Coventryville in 1830, on the assumption that the carver had owned property, probably could be done using maps and deeds of the time, but this approach would be inordinately time consuming and a shot in the dark. Currently, the identity of the Open Urn Man carver remains unknown.

<u>Lettering / Numbers / Identifiers</u>

Most of Open Urn Man's inscriptions begin with a very large "**I**" and complimentary "**n**"; for "Here lies" the "**H**" is either large script, or noted with a sway-bar cross line; some capital "**D**" are in script form; the lower case "**g**" rests entirely above the imagined line; lower case "**w**" has a center bar; lower case "**y**" displays double button terminals; ligature "**Aet**" is the abbreviated Latin form of "**Aetatis**" (at the age of); the "**2**" is another double button form in a "kneeling" position; "**4**" the triangle is large and rests on the line; tear drop "**7**"; "**9**" and "**6**" are mirror forms with a button terminal; abbreviations are often over a "comma" or a dash line over two dots; spiral finial has flat ends. The most unique form is the **Ampersand** which uses the long, left-curved tail.

<u>Open Urn Man Characteristics</u>:

- **Large monuments**, **deeply carved** inscriptions and epitaphs, i.e. 40" to 60" height
- Large **URN** in tympanum, some without interior decoration
- The pseudonym does not reflect the carver's exquisite vines and flower designs.
- **"In"** engraved exceptionally large to introduce inscriptions
- **"In Memory of"** introduces most inscriptions
- When **"Here lies"** is used the "**H**" has a sway-bar mid-line or is in script form
- Large, heavily scored **LEAVES** carved from a left positioned tree trunk
- A **TOMB** with pointed or round top, some with decoration
- **Birds**
- Capital "**W**" sometimes with flourishes
- "Walking the Chisel" format is wide open like a capital **"W."** Coffin Man's is more narrowly spaced.

<u>Territory Range:</u>

East - Old Village Cemetery, Delhi; Old Hamden Cemetery, Hamden; Paige Cemetery, Downsville – all in Delaware Co., NY
West - Center Lisle Cemetery (Maple Shade), Center Lisle, Broome Co., NY
North - Ten Broeck Cemetery, Oxford, Chenango Co., NY; Cincinnatus, Cortland Co., NY
South - Sheshequin Valley, Wysox Church, Wyalusing, Laceyville, Lynn, Tunkhannock, New Milford and Harford – all in Bradford, Susquehanna & Wyoming Counties, PA, generally along Rt. 6 west/east

Cemeteries of Interest:

- **NY - Coventryville Cmty, Coventryville**, Chenango Co., 38 stones; (Stewart - 18, Eclectic Man - 2)
- **NY - Pioneer Cmty, Sidney**, Delaware Co., 6 stones; (Stewart - 8)
- **NY - Riverside Cmty, Whitney Point**, Broome Co., 5 very good stones; (Stewart, Eclectic Man)
- **NY - Upper Lisle Cmty**, **Upper Lisle**, Broome Co., 7 stones; (Eclectic Man)

- **PA - Harford & New Milford**, 9 stones; (Stewart - 15)
- **PA - Sheshequin Valley** 4+; **Cole Cmty, Monroeton** 11; **Towanda** 4 very good; **Wysox Church** 9; **Wyalusing** 7; **Lacey St. Cmty** 8; **Lynn Cmty** 20 (near Springville) **Old Brooklyn** 5; **Franklin Hills Cmty** 11 (West & above Great Bend)
- **PA - Laceyville**; Most remarkable specimens of carver's work

Abigail Bragg d. 1823
Village Cemetery
Lisle, Broome Co., NY

Polly Whiting d. 1822
Smithville Flats Cemetery
Smithville Flats, Chenango Co., NY

Gould Bacon d. 1821
Pioneer Cemetery
Sidney, Delaware Co., NY

PART FIVE

ECLECTIC MAN: APPRENTICE OR COLLABORATOR?

2020

Finally, I would like to bring attention to a possible second apprentice of JW Stewart also known as "Coffin Man." In my 1987 thesis, I brought Eclectic Man into the discussion of artisans whose work is seen across the Southern Tier of New York State. At that time, I had observed only seven local examples of this carver's work and striking samples they were! As the years progressed, I located over one-hundred and thirty similar gravestones and I entertained the possibility that he too, was a product of the Stewart Shop at Coventryville. I invite the reader to revisit my thesis analysis of the work by a gravestone carver I named "Eclectic Man." Much in that commentary about this carver remains true today.[48]

Long before my in-depth search for the identity of local gravestone carvers, a story was brought to my attention about a turncoat Hessian soldier named John Frank who was buried under a gravestone with a unique epitaph. Visiting the Old Virgil Cemetery on Church Street in the Town of Virgil, Cortland County, New York, I easily located the substantial gravestone for this Revolutionary War soldier. Frank's 1830 sandstone marker told of his German birth and immigration, and his epitaph reads, *"Sons of Freedom! Remember liberty is the dread of Monarchs. Tyrants will seek to destroy it. Let the valor of your fathers teach you how to achieve it and their forbearance how to preserve it."*[49] Among the surrounding gravestones I also observed three smaller markers dated 1806, 1813 and 1824. They were embossed with moderately inscribed urns, horizontal coffins, multiple trees, vines and flowers and a distinct lettering style. Who was the carver of these early stones? I made a mental note while on that visit to see if the carver of the three smaller tombstones was a local Virgil resident. Life interrupted.

Eliza Pierce d. 1824
Old Dryden Village Cemetery
Dryden, Tompkins Co., NY

A decade later, while visiting the Texas Valley Cemetery, also located in Cortland County, I noted vertical coffins on more than a dozen memorials. My research has determined these to be the work of JW Stewart. Revisiting the Virgil coffin stones, I compared the designs and inscriptions and determined that the gravestones had not been inscribed by the same artisan. However, I did wonder if the two carvers using the coffin iconography were in some way connected, since their territories overlapped.

---

[48] Dexter, Mary. *Remember Me As You Pass By: The Stone Carvers of Cortland Co., NY*, Interdisciplinary Studies Honors Thesis, University of North Carolina at Chapel Hill, 1987.

[49] Gravestone of John M. Frank. Old Virgil Cemetery, Church St., Virgil, N. Y. tentatively assigned to carver David H. Manrose

Were the carvers related by blood or a shop tradition? I am still unsure as to the answer to that question. Were they master carver and apprentice such as the apparent arrangement between the JW Stewart and the Open Urn carver? Probably not, since the Eclectic Man repertoire was consistently well designed and impressively creative throughout. I feel he is a more mature carver. I have assigned two gravestones in the Coventryville, Chenango County cemetery to Eclectic Man. One, the Benedict stone, is dated 1823 and displays two horizontal coffins on its base and follows Stewart's departure of central New York. They shared time and territory across the Southern Tier of New York State and I wondered what might have been the common thread between them. A few moderate size stones for a Parker family use the Eclectic Man ampersand but seem to be "looks-like" Stewart stones.

My research has disclosed the fact that there is much to suggest that the Eclectic Man's creative and imaginative repertoire includes images that I have seen in the Stewart family's Vermont territory and these give me cause for speculation. They all share:

- The striated body forms
- The extension of finger and toe digits
- Delineated wing lines
- Large, ornate "I" and "N" preceding "In Memory Of"
- Large, ornate interlined "IN"
- A knowledge of the "mask-eye" disc face format, both in profile and full front view

Ann Phelps & child d. 1800
Old South Church Cemetery
Windsor, Windsor Co., VT
By Jonas Stuart of Claremont, NH

I can report that in my extensive travels and years of study, I have not seen one single gravestone in Vermont or New Hampshire that could be said to have been completed by the Eclectic Man carver. However, I propose that he might have seen, and duly noted, the Vermont work of James Grimes Stewart and his father Jonas Stuart. These men all used the aforementioned list of attributes when creating gravestones.

Anderson 1818/1820
Venice Rural Cemetery
Venice, Cayuga Co., NY
By Eclectic Man

Eclectic Man's tympanums predominantly exhibit boldly incised urns with an extended neck displaying hatch marks and a bowl engraved with a broad slash mark which resembles a smiley face. The urn's base, at times, forms a keystone which occasionally drops through an arch that rises from supporting side columns. The preferred incipit is "In Memory of" with special attention paid to the word "IN" which is large and ornately inscribed, often with flecking or slash marks around the lettering. The body of the inscriptions are most often seen within some form of geometric frame i.e. circles, rectangles with corner fans, or ovals. Surrounded by the "walking the chisel" technique, these forms exhibit a distinct and contrasting image within an image. Tulips and curious "peanut" shaped flowers are displayed throughout and shadow lines are seen around capital letters within the inscriptions.

There is no apprentice inventory for Eclectic Man in the Coventryville Cemetery. I have located only a handful of stones that might even be considered "looks-like Stewart" engravings which stand in a close radius of the turnpike hamlet. The two grave markers for the sons of Abiram[*sic*] and Esther Mills found at Guilford Center Cemetery, Chenango County, New York would fill that niche.

Andrew Lunger d. 1827
Van Nortwick Cemetery
Dryden, Tompkins Co., NY

Eclectic Man's inventory moved primarily westward after JW Stewart left the area; however, there is evidence that the former returned to the eastern counties to produce a single marker from time to time, such as the gravestone for Victorine Wheeler buried at Old Village Community Cemetery, Hancock, Delaware County, New York. Two thirds of his inventory is found west of the Tioughnioga River[50] in Tompkins and Cayuga Counties. Found in the isolated Van Nortwick Family Cemetery, Town of Dryden, the Andrew Lunger stone dated 1827 is apparently among his last engraving efforts. Of course, other stones, being backdated, could also be included among his last products, but I have found no stones dated after 1827. There is a small quantity of stones in southern Cayuga County that were prepared and decorated by Eclectic Man; however, these were lettered by an unknown and unnamed carver. These artifacts are dated 1830 through 1832.

I have not discovered gravestones by this carver north of the Cayuga County Towns of Locke, Venice or Sempronius and his inventory within these towns is impressive both in quantity and quality. There is much to suggest that the artisan may have resided in that area or in the northern Tompkins County towns of Groton or Lansing. Unless he was deceased, his name surely appears in southern Cayuga County or Tompkins County in the 1830 Federal Census. This, of course, presumes that our carver owned property and was the Head of Household and not just a digit in someone else's renumeration.

Eliza Pierce d. 1824
Pioneer Cemetery
Dryden, Tompkins Co., NY

A potential hint of his identity appears on two gravestones set many miles apart. Eclectic Man carved the Eliza Pierce stone in Dryden, New York and on the lower left there is the form of a grave marker containing the initials "E P." In Nichols, New York stands the gravestone for Edward Platt with the initials "E P" carved into a tomb image in the tympanum. As you might point out the obvious – both of the deceased's names contain the "E P" initials. The peculiar angle to this puzzle is that in my inventories that include thousands of stones, these are the only two markers that display initials! Did a carver with the initials "E P" tease with these two markers, suggesting in an abbreviated abstract form who he might have been? The Pierce stone is the unquestioned work of

---

[50] Tioughnioga River runs north to south through Cortland County before connecting to the Susquehanna River basin system at the Pennsylvania - New York State line.

Eclectic Man; however, the Platt stone is more ambiguous and may or may not be the work of this same carver. Maybe when reviewing the 1830 Cayuga County census we might investigate residents in the county's southern towns for an "E P."

Lettering / Numbers / Identifiers

Capital letters are **shadow lined** and **"IN" is engraved with large**, **ornate scrolling and set off with flecking.** The top of the **"2" and "9" are tightly wound**; the **"4" cross line** is seen with a **deeply struck terminal**. The **ampersand** is the modified "**U" form with the left leg straight**, at times finished with a left hook; "**aet" and "Aet"** are used and both are in **ligature form**. He sometimes displays a horizontal coffin. Often engraves what can be depicted as "**peanut flowers."**

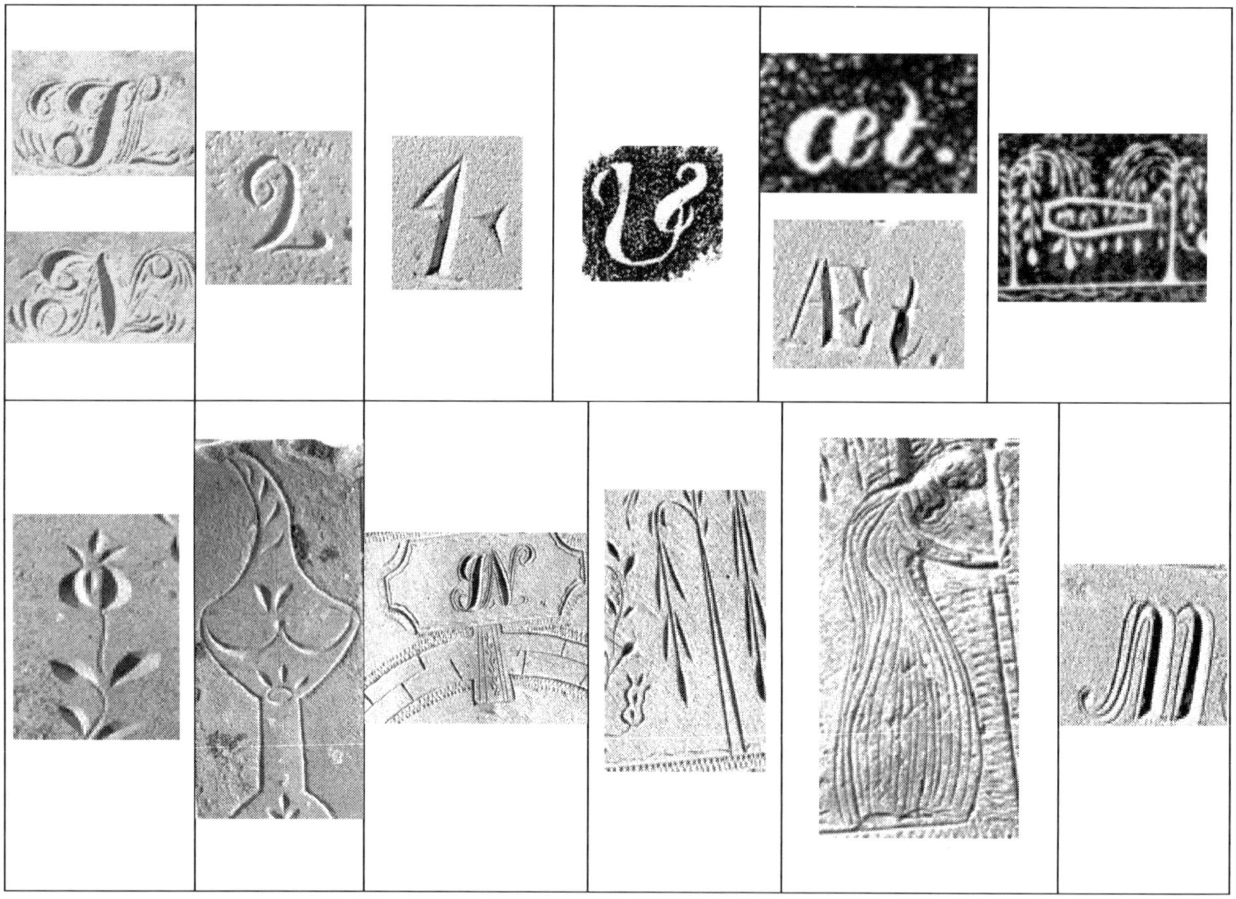

Eclectic Man Characteristics

- **Smiley face urns** top most of his stones
- **Keystones** anchor an arch supported by side columns. Sometimes the foot of an urn
- **Double-lined tree trunks** for the willows
- **Flower forms** are prolifically engraved all across the stones
- **Coffins are always horizontal** though not many in number
- **Descending willow branches** unerringly fall in front of the image

Territory Range in NY

East - Andes Cemetery, Andes, Delaware Co.
Southeast - Revolutionary War Cemetery, Deposit, Delaware Co.
South - Riverside Cemetery, Endicott, Broome Co.
West - Asbury Cemetery, Lansing, Tompkins Co.; Colonel Lindsley Burying Ground, Lindley, Steuben Co.
North - Venice Rural Cemetery (Stewarts Corners), Venice Center and Kelloggsville Cemetery, Kelloggsville, Cayuga Co.

Cemeteries of Interest

- **Center Lisle Cemetery (Maple Shade), Center Lisle**, Broome Co., NY: 9 stones - (1807 backdated-1825) Best complete series of undamaged work
- **Asbury Cemetery, Lansing**, Tompkins Co., NY: 6 stones - (1817-1824)
- **Monaghan/Murphy Cemetery, Locke**, Cayuga Co., NY: 6 stones - (1806-1825)
- **Venice Rural Cemetery (Stewarts Corners), Venice Center**, Cayuga Co., NY: 4 stones - (1815-1825)
- **Venice Center Cemetery, Venice Center**, Cayuga Co., NY: 2 stones - (1822-1826)
- **Lyons Cemetery, Windsor**, Broome Co., NY: 5 stones - (1820-1824) Some of his best work can be seen here.

Stone Characteristic: Gray/brown sandstone, half the stones up to 30 inches above ground, half the stones 40 to 52 inches above ground and 1.5 to 2 inches thick.

SUMMARY.

I have shied away from using the qualifiers "never" and "always" when describing a carver's work on stone. This has brought to light some gravestones that give me pause when attempting to assign the work to a particular artisan. I approach a stone in a graveyard and its initial visual shape will suggest a certain engraver; however, the design or the lettering may look somewhat odd and you begin to question the tympanum and border design that does not seem to match up with the expected letter engraving. These circumstances suggest that the work be assigned to a miscellaneous "Looks-like" category.

Henry Redington d. 18??
Rest Cemetery
Sayre, Bradford Co., PA
"Looks-like" stone

Abigail Car(e)y d. 1820
Eastside Cemetery
Afton, Chenango Co., NY
"Looks-like" stone

Ebenezer Strong d. 1821
Old Athens Cemetery
Athens, Bradford Co., PA
"Looks-like" stone

The early work of Open Urn Man and Eclectic Man, in many instances, seems to be nearly indistinguishable from that of JW Stewart. Open Urn Man mimicked the tympanum images and lettering on smaller stones like those of his mentor. Eclectic Man may also have been involved in producing similar markers. Often, we see both carver's work on the same stone. Even to the trained eye, it can be difficult to differentiate the early work among the Coffin Man group.

Backdated memorials also became quite common as families acquired hard currency and could compensate a trained stone engraver to mark the grave lying beneath field stones. This creates confusion if one tries to solely rely on dates to determine the carver's identity. Both Open Urn Man and Eclectic Man appear to have produced "looks-like Stewart" markers by inscribing lettering details on a quantity of Stewart prepared blanks that already had tympanum work done and were left in the Coventryville shop when he departed the area in 1822. After that time both Open Urn Man and Eclectic Man expressed an individual, unmistakable, personal style that relieves the observer of engaging in further guesswork. Each carver's grave markers truly become a delight to discover.

We continue to search for the exact identity of Stewart's protégés. However, that detail does not prevent us from appreciating the talent, creativity, and hard work of these long-forgotten artisans and their exciting contribution to the local folk art they left behind across the Southern Tier of New York State and northern Pennsylvania in the early nineteenth century.

This project has provided me with a lifetime of research and discoveries. There are many, many more gravestone carvers to kindle the spark that will send you off on such a journey. I have met the most interesting folks in graveyards, both near and far, and have enjoyed hearing their stories about a certain project or that special gravestone or their particular interest in a particular gravestone carver. I look forward to meeting up with you as we are both traversing a cemetery and we can share that something special that has caught our attention. And to think that all this was produced by what I thought was a simple question – who carved those vertical coffins on a stone in Texas Valley, New York?

Mary L. Dexter

CONCLUSION

October 2020

James McCullough d. 1827
Foster Cemetery
Norwich, Chenango Co., NY

Of the original five gravestone carvers surveyed in the Honor's Thesis (1987), two have been identified: "Coffin Man" - Jonas W. Stewart, 2nd discussed extensively in this book, and "Furn Man" - Joseph L. Crandall of Norwich, Chenango County, New York. As I originally hypothesized, further detective work has uncovered the work of "Sunburst Man" in Litchfield, Connecticut. Perhaps one day, we will discover the carver's name is, in fact, James Pettit.

"Open Urn" has now become a standout carver and part of the Stewart Shop. We hope, that as the result of ongoing research, by persons such as yourself, a signed or a probate stone is still out there to produce a given name for the unnamed carvers below. As our field work continues, the territories and inventories continue to expand for these six carvers.

"Coffin Man" - Jonas W. Stewart, 2nd	= 418	gravestones (NY, PA, VT, NH)
"Furn Man" - Joseph L. Crandall	= ?	gravestones (inventory not taken) (NY)
"Sunburst Man"	= 18	gravestones (NY, CT)
"Eclectic Man"	= 132	gravestones (NY)
"Comma Man"	= 54	gravestones (NY)
"Open Urn Man"	= 320	gravestones, to include marble (NY, PA)

Once Jonas W. Stewart, 2nd was identified, as a result of finding a probate file receipt, ongoing research led us to a family of artisans that included his father Jonas Stuart of Claremont, New Hampshire, and a brother James Grimes Stewart of Claremont, New Hampshire and Cabot, Vermont. It has been determined that both of these carvers died and are buried in Center Cemetery, Cabot, Vermont. Their inventories and territories also continue to expand.

Jonas Stuart, [Sr]	= 1,573	gravestones (NH, VT, MA)
James Grimes Stewart	= 417	gravestones (VT, NH)

This project has spanned forty-five years. I have only touched on a few of the many carvers found throughout central New York State. By the 1850s all these skilled and creative artisans of sandstone and marble had been relegated to the pages of history. Many individuals have enriched this research through their curiosity and commentary and suggestions which I hope has assured that a significant body of eighteenth and nineteenth century engraved art has been recognized and recorded. Nearly three thousand gravestones have been surveyed and it is not possible to attach that record to this publication. A print out of the current inventories will be included in the "Stewart" file at the Cortland County Historical Society, Cortland, New York to report on each carver's current inventory and where the stones have been located.

If this story has stimulated your curiosity, I hope to meet you in a cemetery. ~MLD

MAPS

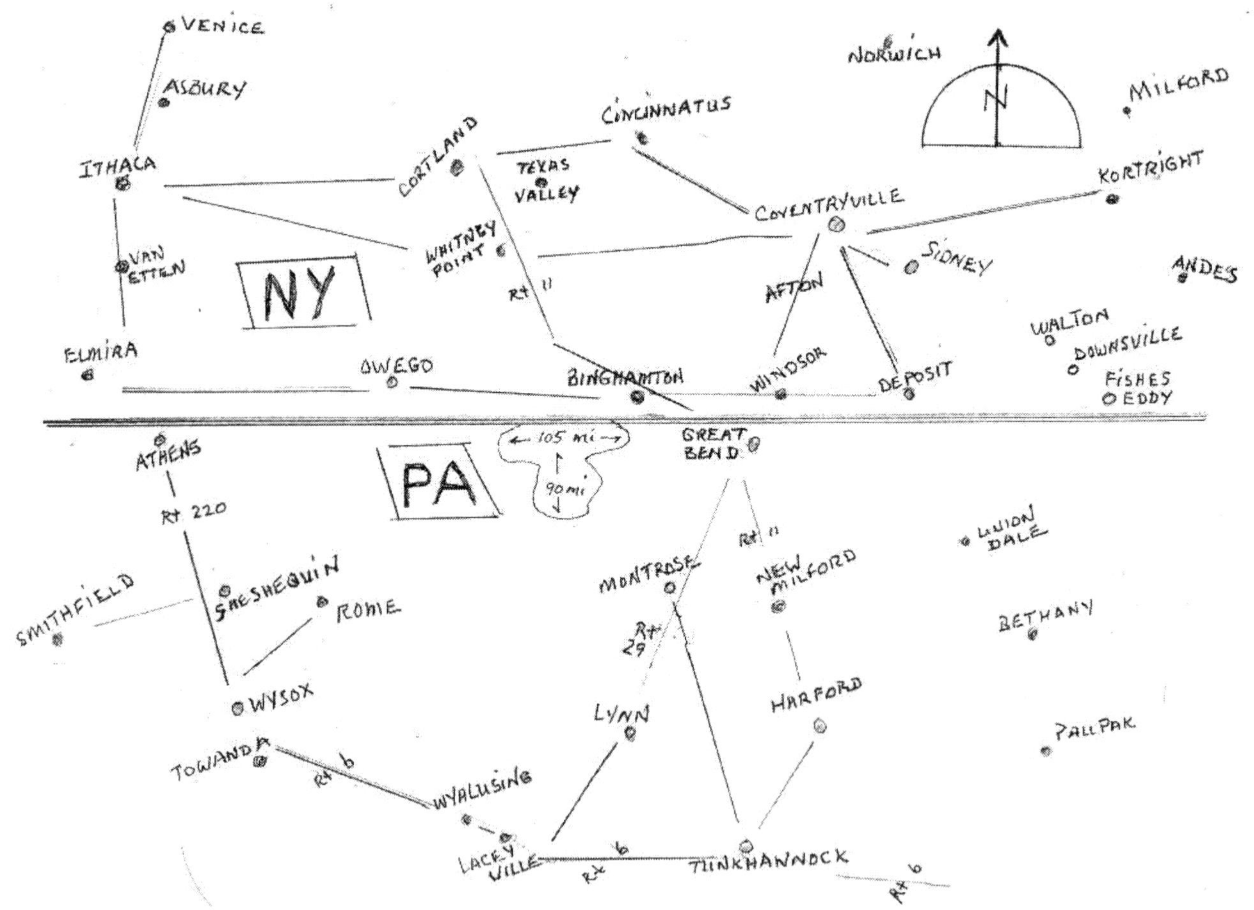

DIAGRAM 1: Disbursement of Coffin Man Group Carvers Work in NY and PA

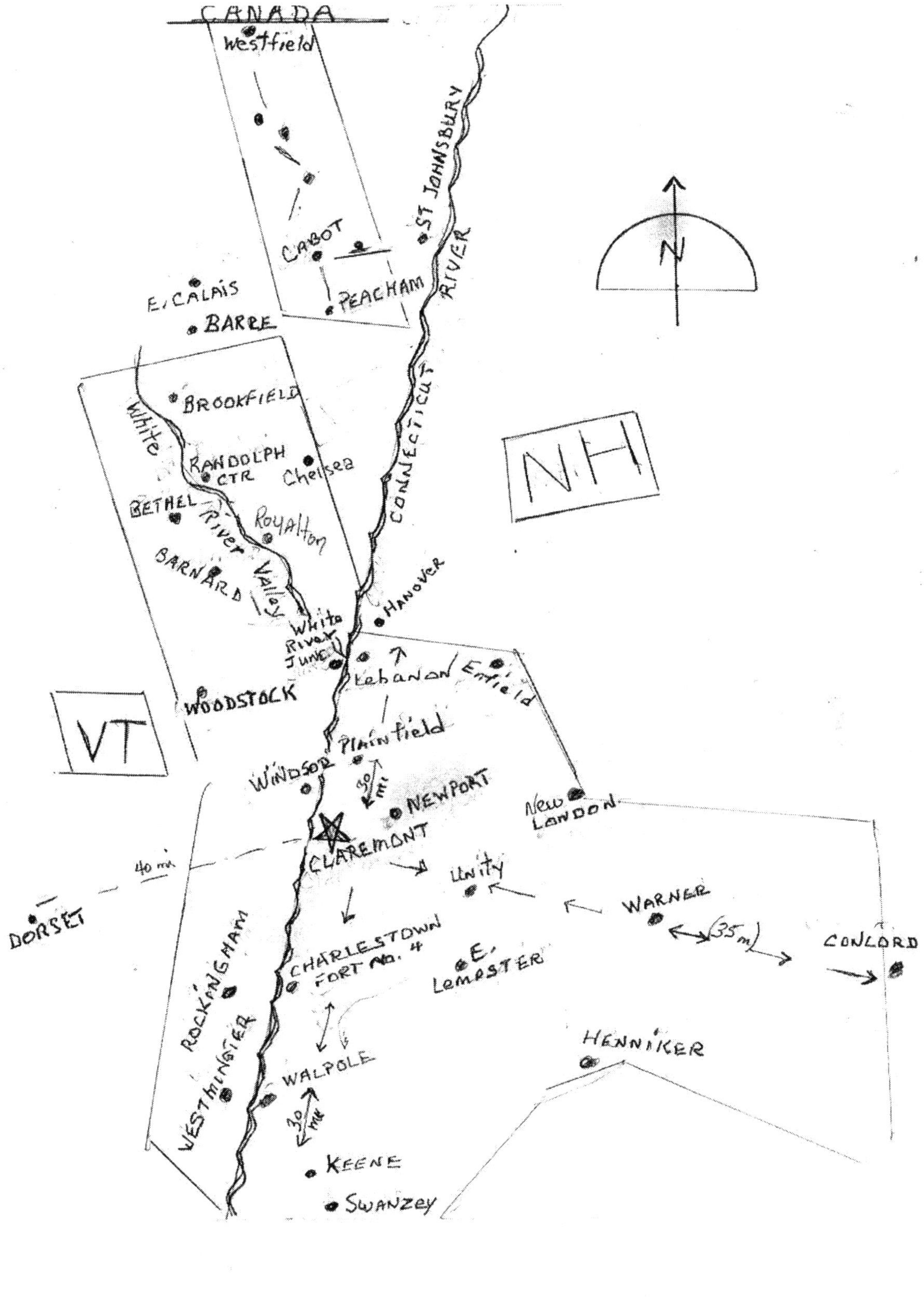

DIAGRAM 2: Disbursement of Stuart/Stewart Family Carvers in Vermont and New Hampshire

ABOUT THE AUTHOR

Mary L. Dexter is a native of Cortland, New York, a place her ancestors immigrated to in the 1860s. She received an AAS degree from Lenoir Community College, Kinston, North Carolina in 1984, and a BA in History with an Afro-American focus from the University of North Carolina at Chapel Hill in 1987. Her Honor's Thesis was entitled "Remember Me As You Pass By, The Early Gravestone Carvers of Cortland County, NY."

An avid genealogist and historian, Mary is a member of the Cortland County Historical Society, Glen Haven Historical Society, Chenango County Historical Society and was a past Cortland City Historian. A longtime member of the Association for Gravestone Studies, she has devoted her life to "furthering the study and preservation of gravestones" which is the mission statement of the organization.

She continues to be passionate and determined in her lifelong quest for knowledge. Mary is always willing to educate folks by sharing her extensive knowledge, and has done numerous presentations and tours on gravestone carvers.